Praise for

friends, followers and Customer Evangelists...

The book is great. It's very well written and is first and foremost unpretentious which is paramount when dealing with a new innovation. I like the textbook feel to it (and yes, I like textbooks! Wanna fight about it? ☺) and of course the step-by-step instructions that, while very useful, don't assume the reader is completely clueless. I think this is a great primer for a business owner who wants to get their feet wet in the Social Media pool.

Adrian Newman
Marketing Director, Lombardi Publishing

Anyone nowadays who is going to be using social media, and the Golden Trio, must read this book. It gives outstanding, easy to understand, easy to read, easy to follow and act upon – all the things about social media and specifically the Golden Trio. A very good, very useful book.

Steven Burda, MBA
President, Burda Consulting
LinkedIn Super Networker

If you want to know what lies beyond Facebook, Twitter, and LinkedIn; Conrad Hall has been there and he's telling the story.

Wayne Stonestreet
Copywriter

Conrad gives us a terrific guide to start-up your business. Using social media accurately is the only way to exist in today's world. This guide helps individuals and professionals organize a huge amount of tools to incorporate in wide range of different marketing strategies.

Ricardo Andorinho
Author of *Awaken Your Genius*

For someone like me, with relatively little experience, the material demystified social networking.

I also found the links and references very helpful. I will definitely be going through the material at least two or three more times as I organize my social networking efforts.

Malcolm Smith
AWAI Instructor

It is just fantastic! What an amazing resource you have created for individuals who are interested in social media.

I think that many people are very overwhelmed with social media, yet understand that it is a very powerful business tool.
Kudos to you!

Jessica Swanson
Shoestring Marketing

There's so much packed in here, it's practically an encyclopedia of social media!

Tim Clay, EA
Accounting and Business Consultants Inc.

Conrad Hall has created the perfect step-by-step, hold-you-by-the-hand guide to help businesses and solopreneurs understand where and how to begin in Social Media.

' *friends, followers & Customer Evangelists* ' is chock full of resources and niche-social sites to help build your business. If you follow Conrad's advice, you'll be up and running without being overwhelmed by the vast choices in today's Social Media scene."

Kathleen Cleary
Boomer Marketing Copywriter

Reading Conrad Hall's *friends, followers & Customer Evangelists* revealed a side of the Internet that I didn't know existed.

Not only does he identify sites that can be of immediate use to you and your business, he show you, step by step, how to use them. In fact, I had both the book and my web browser open, and made immediate improvements to several of my sites following Conrad's directions.

I'd say that anyone using *friends, followers & Customer Evangelists* will save at least 100 hours of their time.

Kevin Adam
CopyCopia Marketing, LLC

friends, followers, and Customer Evangelists

Other Titles by Conrad Hall

Writing E-Books for Fun and Profit
(http://bit.ly/8H25E4)
An e-book is the ideal product to sell on the Internet.
And now, you can create your first e-book ... and start
making money by selling it online ... in 90 days or less.

The Instant Amazon Bestseller Formula
(http://bit.ly/7H1OZK)
Now, whether you're a writer, consultant, coach, speaker,
entrepreneur, executive, or information marketer, you can
get your book on Amazon's top 10 best-seller lists this year.

Building Your Copywriting Website
(http://bit.ly/4KpBQv)
Why reinvent the wheel? Follow my proven formula
for building or updating a Web site for your freelance
copywriting business that: positions you as an expert ...
generates a constant flow of sales leads online ... and helps
clients make the decision to hire you to write for them.

Internet Marketing Over 50
(http://bit.ly/8gH4Rk)
Whether you're already retired or approaching retirement,
Internet marketing is the ideal home business for earning
an extra $175,000+ a year in your spare time.

friends, followers, and Customer Evangelists

The 2010 Business Owner's Guide to Social Media

CONRAD HALL

New York

friends, followers, and Customer Evangelists
The 2010 Business Owner's Guide to Social Media

Conrad Hall Copywriting, LLC

410-250 Cassandra Blvd
Toronto, ON M3A 1V1
Canada

5204 Bessemer Super Hwy
Brighton, Al 35020
United States

561-623-9441
conrad@theconradhall.com

ISBN 978-1-60037-742-6

Library of Congress Control Number: 2009943573

Morgan James Publishing
1225 Franklin Ave., STE 325
Garden City, NY 11530-1693
Toll Free 800-485-4943
www.MorganJamesPublishing.com

Cover Design by: 3 Dog Design
www.3dogdesign.net

In an effort to support local communities, raise awareness and funds, Morgan James Publishing donates one percent of all book sales for the life of each book to Habitat for Humanity. Get involved today, visit **www.HelpHabitatForHumanity.org.**

In Memory Of

Grandma Charters
    You taught me to love writing

and

Aunt Geri
    You loved me like a son, and
    showed me the joy of learning

"Take time to deliberate, but when the time for action has arrived, stop thinking and go in."

-- Napoleon Bonaparte

The time for action truly is now. In 2010, any business not actively working to integrate social networking and video with their existing advertising is falling behind their competitors.

That's bad enough, but what's worse is that they are not listening to their customers. Customers want to interact with you, and be heard. Social Media is the tool they have chosen for doing this.

"A journey of a thousand miles begins with a single step."

-- Confucius

Equation Research says the single biggest problem facing business owners who want to use social media is "not knowing enough to even get started." You want to take that first step, but aren't sure where to put your foot.

The 2010 Business Owner's Guide to Social Media is your first step. Take it with confidence.

Preface

The idea for *friends, followers and Customer Evangelists* came while I was learning to use social media myself. It's my fifth "how-to" book, so I have some sense of what is useful to my audience.

You can see how it would occur to me that questions I had while getting started in social media would be similar to questions you're having now. That's when I started making notes and planning this book.

The research for *friends, followers and Customer Evangelists* was done by going to the sites, becoming a member and making use of the tools. Some of the results I've had are:

- ✓ Increasing traffic to my website by 782%
- ✓ Being invited to sponsor the Community Marketing Blog's Blog Off Competition
- ✓ Obtaining a mainstream publisher for this book
- ✓ Raising my monthly revenues by 280%

There are dozens of reviewers who have looked at the manuscript and given their encouragement and feedback. Some spotted broken links, others spotted spelling and grammar mistakes, and one sharp reader spotted an error in the video sites section. One of the site descriptions had been missed, and it caused all the rest to be with the wrong site name.

This book would never have been completed without the support and encouragement of four dedicated friends. Yvette Pacheco, who did the editing and has also become the most important person in my life. Tim Clay who is my accountant, friend, and trusted advisor. Wayne Stonestreet, a man of incredible depth and perception who also happens to be a technical wizard. And David Hancock – without his encouragement, I would never have submitted the manuscript for publication.

Without David's encouragement, I would never have met people like Lyza Poulin, Rick Frishman and Jim Howard. It is the team at Morgan James Publishing that deserves credit for making this dream a reality.

And thank you to you, the reader. Any book is useless while it sits on a shelf. It is your willingness to take action and enjoy success that gives true fulfillment to *friends, followers and Customer Evangelists*.

To help you make the most of this book, I'd like you to have a digital copy of it. You'll see as you read that *friends, followers & Customer Evangelists* is filled with hyperlinks (the underlined, blue lettering).

Obviously you can't "click on a link" when you're holding the book, but this book is most effective when you can use the links. The answer is simple: Give you an electronic copy to go with this print version.

Just go to www.TheConradHall.com/loyaltycopy.

When you type that URL (web address) into your browser, it's going to take you straight to a digital copy of this book. No landing page, no sales hype – just the book.

I suggest you save a copy to your hard drive so you can take it with you anywhere. Then you can read the print version, make notes, and highlight points while you use the electronic version (e-book) to access all the links and resources.

Also check out the Video Training Bonus mentioned on the cover. Just flip to page 19 for more details.

Please do take a minute to send me an e-mail, too (conrad@ theconradhall.com). Let me know how this book helps you, what you'd like to see added, and what I can do to be of further service to your business success. Thank you for being a reader.

Sincerely,
Conrad Hall
16 December 2009

Table of Contents

Introduction

Social Media has become THE marketing tool of the 21st century.

There are hundreds of books, videos and audio recordings telling you how to:

- ✓ make money with Twitter
- ✓ get top ratings on YouTube
- ✓ use LinkedIn to get a job or more clients

But none of them tells you about the hundreds of other social media sites that are out there – until now.

It's wonderful that social media is getting attention, and that marketers are waking up to the need for treating customers like people instead of cash cows. But have you noticed that when everybody's focused on the same thing – it gets real hard to be heard?

Facebook, Twitter, LinkedIn, and all the other "big name" social media sites are good tools. You should make use of them. But there are other social media sites you can make use of that are niche-focused.

LibraryThing.com is one example. This site is for book-lovers (in case the name didn't give it away) and it offers a lot of functionality as well as the opportunity to connect with other people. A site like this is ten times better than finding a book group on one of the mammoth social media sites.

The only reason people are going to LibraryThing.com is because they enjoy books. They aren't looking for the latest music video, surfing current events, or tweeting about what they did at work today. They're at LibraryThing.com because they want to find books, talk about books, or share their opinions on books.

You can see how someone who offers talking books, sells rare books, or makes custom book jackets is well served by knowing about this site.

Well, that's the one thing I see missing – where to find the hundreds of other social media sites where it's easy to be heard and the users are in a niche market. That's the reason for creating this guide.

1

There are 357 sites listed in this guide. That's a lot more marketing and networking opportunities than the half dozen or so sites you're hearing about in all the how-to manuals. Plus, I've listed several services – in addition to the social media sites – that help you coordinate your social media.

Services like Ping.fm, Tweetdeck, and FriendFeed. These services save you hours of effort by automating tasks.

To give you a roadmap for getting involved with social media, let's move on to the next section and look at the Social Media QuickStart.

Social Media QuickStart

1. Join the Golden Trio
Start your social media marketing efforts off by being part of Facebook, Twitter, and LinkedIn. These three give you the most exposure and will bring you a steady stream of new contacts. Smaller, niche-focused social media sites will bring you lower traffic volumes but with the higher conversion rates (produces more sales) that go with niche marketing.

2. Complete Your Profiles
Starting with the Golden Trio also gives you an incredible resource just by completing your profile for each one. These sites give you the most complete opportunities to describe yourself, and your business, possible. Take advantage of it so you can just copy and paste information into your profile for other social media sites, an Author's Resource Box for article marketing, and even press releases when you need a quick bio.

3. Join Niched Social Media Sites
Look through the sites listed in this guide and join those related to your market and your interests. Everything you do to build a presence in the Golden Trio can be re-purposed into building a presence on the smaller, niche-market sites.

4. Connect with Friends
You might be surprised how many of your friends are already on social media sites – and even by how many aren't. Invite your friends to connect with you on each site you join. Those who are already involved with social media are a good resource for you to learn from, and those who aren't involved are a good resource to help you grow by sharing what you learn.

5. Connect with Role Models
Find the people who are leaders in your market and connect with them. Being connected gives you access to the conversations in which they

participate – and that can be a priceless education. Connecting with them is also a good way to have something to talk about when you meet them at a conference.

6. Answer Questions

Some sites have Q&A sections where you can post answers and be rated for how useful your answer is. Other sites, like Twitter, will simply have questions come up in the natural course of online conversations. Either way, answering questions shows you have something to contribute and that you're actively participating in the community.

7. Ask Questions

Answering a question is how you give to the online community. Asking a question is how you take. Everyone knows you should give before you take. If there's an FAQ (Frequently Asked Questions) section on the site, be sure to check it before posting your question. Asking a common question that has been answered repeatedly will, at best, get you the suggestion to check the FAQ page. At worst, it can bring you scathing comments and ridicule.

8. Connect with Prospects

Being involved in the online conversations will help you discover who has a need for your product or service. It will also show everyone else what your knowledge and expertise is – and your prospects will come to you. This is the goldmine Jim explains in *Social Networking* – how to use social media effectively enough so customers come calling on you.

1. How to Use This Guide

This guide is your primary reference for developing and guiding your social media marketing plan.

In the text, appendices, and site listings are the tools and references you need to use social media as an effective, profitable advertising medium for your business. There are links to dozens of books, websites and videos sprinkled throughout the pages of this guide that will lead you to being a social media professional – if that is your goal.

Before you get started reading, please take a second to visit www.TheConradHall.com/loyaltycopy.

This web address opens an electronic copy of this book in your browser. It's yours free for having purchased a copy of this book. Save that electronic copy to your hard drive so you can read and highlight this print version while you use the electronic version (e-book) to access the links and resources.

For the typical business owner – the person whose time is stretched to the max – this guide serves as a guide and check to your own efforts, or as a companion to help you with outsourcing the work to a social media professional.

The guide is split into three categories:
1. Social Networking
2. Social Bookmarking
3. Video Sharing

Between the categories are chapters to give you more information about how to make the best use of each kind of site.

The social networking sites are first because this is where you'll start. In fact, you should start specifically with Facebook and Twitter. The profiles for these two site are easy to set up (Twitter takes about 17 seconds to complete), and Facebook is primarily a social site. If you're a little slow filling in some of the areas of your profile, then it won't matter as much on Facebook.

Facebook also offers the best selection of tools to go with a social media site. It's a good place to practice uploading photos, video, files, sending messages and joining groups. As long as you're being polite, and uploading content you're comfortable with the world seeing, you'll be just fine "learning the ropes" with Facebook.

The first thing to do on Twitter is look for role models. Who are the people in your industry that you want to emulate? Look for them on Twitter and follow them so you can see what they're doing on a daily basis.

You should also visit www.MrTweet.com. This is a site that specializes in finding people you'll be glad to follow – people in your industry who are active on Twitter.

Once you're signed-up for Facebook and Twitter, be sure to use the "add friends" and "find people" functions to connect with people you know. Starting with your friends is a good, comfortable way to start building your network. As you progress, you'll start meeting new people and make new friendships. Some will be in your industry, and some won't. Be sure you're meeting both kinds of people because you never know what new and exciting things a stranger can introduce to your life.

On that note, let me slide in a brief caution about social media. Avoid putting personal information anywhere on the internet that relates to your finances or identity. Credit cards, driver's licenses, and social security numbers belong in your wallet – not on the net.

Personally, I even have a separate, public e-mail address I use for social media, my blog, the books I write and everything else "public." I don't even use my real birthday when it's requested. All they need to verify is that I'm old enough to agree to their terms and conditions, so I use a day that's in the same year that I was born, but not my real birthday – just to be safe.

Okay, that's enough about safe surfing.

When you have your profiles competed on Facebook and Twitter, the next place to go is into the Groups area on Facebook. Look for groups related to your business, and for groups related to things you enjoy outside of business.

Part of being on social media is showing people your warm, human side. I like taking pictures – some of them even turn out well – and Facebook is the place where I share those photos. They help to show that I'm not a workaholic sitting in front of the computer from morning 'til night every day, and it gives people something to chat with me about other than business.

I enjoy writing – it's more fun than chocolate – but it isn't all there is to my life. And whatever you do certainly is not all there is to your life, either. So make a point of showing your interests when using social media sites.

There are three more sites I recommend visiting and becoming a part of:

✓ LinkedIn – because it's a business networking site filled with opportunities, interesting groups, and inspiring role models.

✓ FriendFeed – because this site lets you collect all your social media action into one place so people who are interested in you can find it easily.

✓ Ping – because social media can quickly take a lot of your time. Ping allows you to update dozens of social media sites all at once.

Each of these sites is listed here in the guide. You can flip over to the Index of Sites to find which page each one is on, and all the site names are hyperlinks. Just click on a site name to open your browser and go straight to the site.

Once you have these sites set up, come back to the guide and browse through the sites listed in each section. As you find sites that appeal to you – whether for business or personal interests – click on the site name and explore it.

What you're looking for are the niche sites. They have smaller audiences that are on that site because they have a specific interest. Think of each site as a networking opportunity – it's an opportunity for you to help other people and develop relationships. You're planting seeds.

As you get comfortable with using social media and develop a presence, you can be asking and answering questions. Get involved with the various communities and cultivate the contacts you've made.

Think of these sites as being the same as clubs you join in your community. Would you go out and join a bowling league, baseball team, parent-teacher association, and every service club in town? Probably not – you'd never be able to keep up that kind of schedule. Social media is the same way.

You should only participate in sites that genuinely interest you. If you're on a site just because you think it presents a "good market," then that is going to show through. That approach won't take long for you to tarnish the reputation you've built.

Since you're using this guide to find sites that are relevant to you, let me take some time to show you how the sites are organized.

Within each category, the sites are listed with their Google, Alexa, and Compete page rankings.

Remember: The names of the sites are hyperlinks so you can click on any name and visit that site.

How the Page Rankings Work

The rankings used are from Google, Alexa, and Compete.

The page rankings from Google, Alexa, and Compete are objective.

Page Rankings (PR) from Google peak at 10. (I've only seen two pages with a 10. One was for Google's Notebook, but Google has stopped providing this service. The other is for Google Talk.) Each site with a Google PR of 4 or higher has a text description with it.

The text description is part of a subjective rating. It tells you what the site does, and what the target market for the site is plus a little bit more. The length of the text description gives you a strong indication of my opinion of the site. When you see just a few words, you'll know there isn't much that makes the site stand out or seem interesting.

The Page Rankings from Alexa and Compete follow a different pattern from Google. Their best site ranking is a 1, and the rankings go all the way into the millions and tens of millions.

You can see that the rankings from Alexa and Compete have a much finer degree of sorting than what you get from Google. So, when you see a PR in single or double digits from Alexa or Compete, it's really worth paying attention to.

All the rankings for the sites come from www.Popuri.us, and every site's ranking was checked Tuesday, July 7, 2009.

There's significantly more information available from Popuri than what I've included here. Each search shows you how many backlinks a site has from Yahoo, Live Search, and Google. It gives information about the WHOIS registration (who owns the domain), and the links to the site through Technorati and del.icio.us.

So let's take a look at what these numbers from Google, Alexa and Compete actually mean.

What the Page Rankings Mean

The better a page's ranking, the more popular the page is.

But that popularity means more than just having a lot of people visit the site every day. It includes:

- ✓ how often someone bookmarks the site (or any page in the site)
- ✓ whether people are establishing backlinks (or trackbacks) to the site
- ✓ how many inbound and outbound links a site has
- ✓ whether the content is fresh (because you're adding to it regularly)
- ✓ how many of the SEO (Search Engine Optimization) components are actually working together and make sense

The PR for a site is based on how much visitors like it and how much the web spiders like it.

> *Quick Note: A web spider is a program that crawls around the internet looking at sites. It doesn't look at pretty colors or flash videos. It just looks at the criteria given above – plus other things the search engines don't disclose (trade secrets) – and gives the site a grade: the page rank.*

But that doesn't mean a site with a low PR is a bad site. It's a little like keyword search volume. You can use a keyword that has a monthly search volume of 100,000 – and it will give you lots of traffic. Another keyword with a monthly search volume of 7,000 isn't going to give you as much traffic, but that keyword might have a much higher conversion rating.

A site with a lower page ranking will have a lower traffic volume and might not be as well connected to other sites. Yet, the traffic it has could easily be a dedicated following that is ready to hear your message.

For example, Facebook, Twitter, and LinkedIn are the Golden Trio of social media. They're big sites with lots of members, and you should definitely put time into using these three services.

On the other hand, LibraryThing.com is a smaller site that you might not ever have heard of. Or how about Minti.com? These sites have smaller audiences and lower PRs than the Golden Trio, but those audiences are well targeted. It would be a mistake for someone whose business is books to overlook LibraryThing.com, and anyone who markets to parents definitely wants to know about Minti.com.

That means looking through each of the sites listed here to find the ones related to your market. Explore each site you participate in for groups within the site who have a need or desire for what you're providing.

Here's a little bit of my own experience to give you a picture of what I mean.

> *I've been part of LinkedIn, Facebook, and several other social networking sites for about a year. There are a few hundred people with whom I've connected, and we exchange comments once in a while.*
>
> *For the longest time, I wondered what I could do to "be more human" in the internet world. After all, just visiting a site to answer questions and look for business related stuff was boring and, honestly, tedious. It was like going to a convention and talking business the whole time. I wanted to get to know people.*
>
> *One day it dawned on me that I could share my photos. I'm just an amateur photographer, but I truly enjoy being outdoors and taking pictures. It turns out that it's also fun to describe where the photo came from (which park, what it took to get the photo) and even what I did throughout the day.*
>
> *Opening up and sharing my hobby is still quite new to me. It's taking some practice, and I'm learning. The results are already impressive, too.*
>
> *People are commenting on my photos and asking questions. It's generating a dialogue — and that's exactly what I want.*

So, make sure you get involved with each site you participate in. Whether it has a Google PR of 9 or 1 has less impact on the results you get than how well your participation rates.

Now, let's look at the Social Networking sites and how they rate. After them come the Social Bookmarking sites and then the Video Sharing sites.

2. What is Social Networking?

Social networking is our answer to the constant bombardment of advertising. It's the one place where we can actively shut out anyone who comes in shouting his or her marketing message.

Social networking is about finding ways to cooperate – looking for the proverbial "do unto others" situations.

And, finally, social networking is about being social. It's a way to give yourself a face and express your personality in the ultimately un-human world of electrons, Meta tags, and keywords.

Social Networking takes different forms on the Internet. There are mega sites – Twitter, Facebook, and LinkedIn (and their imitators). There are local-focus sites – Meetup and Meetin. And then there are the hundreds of general and niche focused sites like LibaryThing.com and TravBuddy.com.

Add to that mix the millions of blogs, forums, and groups that are on the internet and you can see why more than two-thirds of marketers are using social media already.

Yet even with the wide range of sites and topics covered, there are a few elements that show up on almost every site.

Your Profile

Whether it's as short as your name and e-mail address (for Twitter), or includes a complete history of your employment, interests and ambitions (for LinkedIn), every social site gives you a profile. After all, it's hard to be social if no one knows you who are.

Photos

Part of letting people know who you are in your profile is giving them something to look at – preferably a photo of you. The nice thing about this feature is that most sites allow you to upload more than one photo. Having several photos of yourself lets you change the look of your profile to suit the seasons, holidays, or even just show off your latest vacation.

Status Updates & Comments

We wouldn't be able to call it "networking" if we didn't do anything to stay in touch with one another. Twitter gives you 140 characters (a Tweet) to update people on what you're doing – it's called Tweeting and/or micro-blogging.

Of course, what makes for the social part of all these sites is that you get to comment on what other people are doing. You might "like it," give a thumbs up, or simply type a comment and post it. Whether there is a limit on how long your comment can be depends entirely on which site you're using.

Sites don't always impose a limit on how long you can make an update or comment, but do try to avoid writing a whole letter. There are better ways to communicate at length on a social networking site (SNS).

Messages

This is one of those better ways to communicate a lot of information. The message function on any site is just about the same as sending an e-mail. Facebook (among others) even allows sending attachments with messages – photos, video, gifts, and links to name a few.

Privacy Settings

"We respect your privacy." It's a common slogan on websites – especially when they're asking for your e-mail address. When it comes to an SNS, this is something you should pay attention to because they're not all created equal.

For example, I unsubscribed from one SNS, deleted my profile, "blocked" their e-mails, and sent them an e-mail asking to be removed from their list – all to no avail. It finally took adding them to my "Blocked Senders" list in Outlook to stop seeing their e-mails.

Then there's the issue of privacy while you're on the site.

For starters, you should NEVER put anything <u>on any site</u> that you wouldn't want to see on the cover of a magazine – or on your employer's desk. Aside from that basic principle, there might be something you want to put on a site to share with family and friends that you don't want the world to see. Perhaps photos of your new baby, a birthday party, or other special event.

Always look at a site's privacy options before deciding to make it a social networking "home." There is no standard, so some sites automatically make everything private, others make things public. The best sites, like Facebook and FriendFeed (now owned by Facebook) give you the tools to set your own "basic level" of privacy, and then allow you to make things more, or less, private on an item-by-item basis if you want to.

Groups

Even video sites have groups with different interests, so you'll find this option on just about every social media site – not just the networking sites. Being able to join or form a group allows you to become an expert and a leader in your field of interest. As a business owner, you can see how that's good for your reputation and your business.

In addition to the "mandatory" elements you'll find on all the sites, there are quite a few extras that sites offer. The first one I'll look at is a bit of a strange duck:

Applications

These are often called "Plugins," "Widgets," "Gadgets," and/or "Social Apps." There are, literally, thousands of these little programs available, but they don't work everywhere. Some are designed specifically to work with Twitter, others are for your blog, and some are for your cell phone.

Applications are a bit strange because they can come from anywhere. Some are authored by different sites, but most come from people who are good at programming. They write an application to do a particular task and then make it available to anyone who wants it. It's called "Open Source Coding," and it's just one aspect of social networkers doing good things.

It's also handy to know that the names <u>tend</u> to tell where the application works. (I emphasize <u>tend</u> because these are not hard and fast rules.)

- ✓ Plugins are most often associated with blogs
- ✓ Widgets go with sites like MySpace and Facebook
- ✓ Gadgets seem to have been spawned by Twitter
- ✓ Social Apps could go with anything, but seem to be most often associated with cell phones.

Applications can block spam, add your signature and play music – just like any piece of software you have on your computer. To help you see what they can do, and how they fit in to social media (specifically a blog), click on this link: <u>http://www.michelfortin.</u> <u>com/wordpress-plugins-michel-fortin-blog/</u>.

This takes you to a post Michel wrote that lists all the Plugins he uses on his blog, and what they do. (Definitely bookmark this page so you can refer back to it when setting up or adding to your blog.) There are dozens of applications listed here. A great thing about the description that goes with each application is that you can look around his blog and see how most of the applications (Plugins) are working.

I say "most" because some of them run in the background. For example, one of the Plugins allows you to backup your Wordpress database. That's a maintenance function that you'll never see happening on the blog.

Start with Michel's post so you'll have a better understanding of what applications can do. It makes life easier when you start exploring applications on the social networking sites.

Video

Obviously video is an essential element for YouTube and every other video sharing site, but it's a relatively new addition to Facebook, MySpace and other SNS. That's because video has been hard to handle since there are about a thousand different video formats available on the market today.

The great thing about video is that it's incredibly cheap to produce. You can get a Sony HD video camera for under $200, and some of the free editing software available is truly useful. I know this will sound like me "parroting" other experts – still – marketing sites that aren't using video are, right now, today, at a disadvantage to the sites that are using it.

These are the two "biggest" extra items that sites offer. Are there more? Sure, and I'd be happy to use another 12 or 14 pages to describe them all. But there are other things we need to cover, and I don't want to drown you with information you might never have a use for. There's too much other fun, truly useful, stuff to play with and explore.

One thing I find really cool about social media is that it's only about 8 years old. Even desktop computers didn't impact the world of business this quickly.

Yes, we can go "all the way back" to 1994 and 1995 for TheGlobe.com (Cotriss, David, 05.29.2008), "Where are they now: TheGlobe.com", *The Industry Standard*), Geocities and Tripod. This is when we first saw chat rooms and personalized home pages.

Classmates also appeared in 1995, and SixDegrees.com started in 1997.

MySpace, Friendster and Bebo didn't come along until the 21st Century! Facebook only came onto the scene in 2004 – and it's now arguably the largest and most popular social networking site in the world.

This guide alone lists over 300 mainstream social media sites. That doesn't include the thousands of white label, private social sites hosted by companies or the thousands of other sites developed using services like Ning.com. (Ning sites will have their own section in next year's guide.)

Social Media – networking, bookmarking, blogging, video sharing – is now as permanent a part of our world as newspapers.

It helps to think of social networking as a service club. Joining a site is similar to joining the Rotary Club, Kiwanis, or Lions.

When you join a service club, it's usually because someone invited you. You accept the invitation, introduce yourself (complete your profile), and take some time to get to know people – learn how things work. You do the same things on networking sites.

The same etiquette applies to service clubs and social networks. Other members expect you to give back to the community in return for the opportunity to network and grow your business.

That said, you should start by understanding that social networking is NOT primarily a tool for marketing. Its primary purpose is to connect people on a social level.

Yes, you can use social networking to promote your business. And no, there aren't any rules in place in the same way that the FDA regulates health claims. What is in place is something far more powerful than the regulations any bureaucrat could ever dream up.

The governing force in social networking is your customer.

They don't need to shout from the rooftops or call all the major media networks. When a customer is upset, they just have to sit at their computer and tell their friends.

The first rule of social networking is to be polite. A close second is to be helpful.

Create a reputation for having answers, and prospects will come to you. For example, someone who owns a shoe store could write a blog post or an article that shows 5 reasons why our feet hurt when we wear certain shoes. Or they might write an article about how to make sure your shoes fit properly to keep your feet from hurting.

The point is to share what you know for everyone's benefit.

A common misconception is that everyone will just take what you know, use it and never contact you. Think about that for a second. Do you know how to change the oil in your car? Lots of people do – and even do it – but the oil change shops are all still in business, right?

When you share what you know, it gives other people a chance to see your expertise. Those who take your knowledge and use it are good advertising for you. The others who come and ask for your help are your customers.

And you don't have to be Mark Twain or Hemmingway to share your knowledge. Readers actually like it – even prefer it – when you make occasional spelling mistakes and ignore some of the grammar rules. It makes you human and approachable in this world of experts and gurus.

Just write as if you're talking to a friend at the kitchen table or sitting at a bar.

There is a huge arena of business opportunity for you to explore in social networking.

As you build your online presence, you are going to meet people you want to approach and others are going to discover you. These encounters are going to result in more than just getting new clients. A lot of the people you meet will represent opportunities for joint ventures and affiliate agreements.

To help you be ready to take advantage of joint venture and affiliate opportunities there are two resources I think you'll find useful.

The best resource I've found for planning and executing a joint venture is from Strategic Profits. It's titled *Joint Venture Partnerships Guide* (just click on any blue, underlined text to go to the related website). I'm not going to pull any punches – this guide has a price tag with it. There's a copy as part of my reference library, so I think it's worth it, but you should check it out for yourself.

Read this guide through, make notes and – MOST IMPOR-TANTLY – do the exercises. This guide (*friends, followers and Customer Evangelists*) is a product that's promoted through joint ventures (JVs). Every step of finding, contacting, and working with my JV partners was accomplished using the *Joint Venture Partnership Guide*.

The resource for affiliates – being one or finding them – comes from Ken Evoy and SiteSell.com. Appropriately, it's titled *The Affiliate Master's Course*.

This resource is FREE.

To find *The Affiliate Master's Course*, just scroll down the page this link takes you to (it's the sitemap for SiteSell.com) until you come to the heading **Free Downloads**. It's the third item in the left column.

Be sure to sign up for their affiliate program, too, because they have a terrific educational process in addition to the other resources they provide.

Be sure to print the *Joint Venture Partnership Guide* from Strategic Profits and *The Affiliate Master's Course* from SiteSell.com. Read them both with a pen in hand. Make notes as you read and be sure to take action on what you read.

The most important element of social networking – as with any business activity – is taking action. (That's why it's called an *activity* instead of a *rest period*.)

There are more than 300 sites listed in this guide. You could join every last one and get no more benefit than you're getting right now – if you join and do nothing.

As I mentioned in the Quick Start section, start your social networking by joining the Golden Trio: Facebook, Twitter, and LinkedIn. We walk through creating these profiles, and joining groups, in the next chapter – Getting Started in Social Media.

As you comfortable, find ways to give back to the community and become familiar with the tools listed in Chapter 11 – Coordinate Your Social Media. These tools will help get things done faster, and maximize the time you invest in social media.

Before we move on to look at the social networking sites, let me tell you about one more free resource related to social networking.

Lee LeFever has put together a fun, short (1 min. 48 sec.) video that explains what Social Networking is in plain English. Just visit http://www.commoncraft.com/video-social-networking to watch the video. (You'll find lots of useful videos at Lee's site.)

3. Getting Started in Social Media

Everybody likes Social Media. It's the hot topic of the decade – for now.

But the single biggest barrier for business owners who want to get involved with social media is not knowing where to start. Equation Research published a study in July 2009 that found one third of small business owners just don't know how to get started with social media.

Well, you can imagine my first thought was "Hey, I can fix that. I'm pretty good at explaining things." And that's precisely what I'm doing for you now.

This chapter uses images of all the web pages you're going to encounter with notes added to them. Plus I'm putting explanations into the text. By the time we're finished, you'll have profiles completed for the Golden Trio: Facebook, Twitter and LinkedIn.

Once those profiles are complete, all you have to do is copy and paste whatever you want for any profile on any other social media site. There's even a blank profile sheet for you to make notes on in Appendix D. So let's get started.

Facebook and LinkedIn use a two stage process for completing your profile. When you sign-up they only ask for a little bit of information to make signing up easier. Once you've opened an "account" with them, then you can add more details to your profile.

We're going to mimic that two step process. First we look at how to get accounts with each of the Golden Trio sites, and then we'll walk through all the details of each profile. Then we'll invite friends, find some role models, and connect with people.

So let's get started with making some accounts. If you already have accounts with the Golden Trio sites, you can just skip over this section and go to Finishing Your Profiles on page 38.

Getting Your Accounts

We mentioned **Bonus Video Training** on the cover, and this is where it fits in.

To make sure you get this content in the form that works best for you, I took the time to go through the sign-up process for Facebook, LinkedIn and Twitter a second time. This time, I ran a screen-recording so you could see it happening.

I also narrated what I was doing, and pointed out a few things –points of interest – as I went along. So you have the text here in the book with complete, step-by-step instructions. And you have a video demonstration for each site with audio narration. That should cover just about every learning style.

Here are the URLs (web addresses) for each of the videos:

Facebook: http://bit.ly/8SilUf

LinkedIn: http://bit.ly/5Q7W1T

Twitter: http://bit.ly/5HTPw1

Be sure to type the URLs just as they are printed. An important point to keep in mind is that a URL is case sensitive after the single forward slash. For example, http://Bit.ly and http://bit.ly take you to the same place. But everything that comes after the first forward slash – for any web address – is case sensitive. Type it just the way you see it.

Even better, be sure to visit:

www.TheConradHall.com/loyaltycopy

and get your free digital copy of this book. Then you can just click on the links and get to where you want to go.

If you do have questions after reading this section and watching the videos, please do let me know. I'll be happy to do my best in getting you an answer.

And let me know if you need help with making a plan for using social media. Social media is a great tool, and you can have a lot of fun using it. It can bring you a lot of success, but it's also huge – there are over 300 sites in this guide alone!

Having a plan before you get started is critical to making the best use of your time and resources. At the very least, you should write down:

✓ What you want to achieve

✓ Which sites you'll use

✓ What you'll do on each site to achieve the goals you set

Of course, that's what this guide is all about. You'll see more about planning your social media efforts in Chapter 5.

Let's get started with creating your accounts, and remember to watch the videos.

Twitter

Let's start with Twitter because it's the easiest. Here's what you see when you go to Twitter.com.

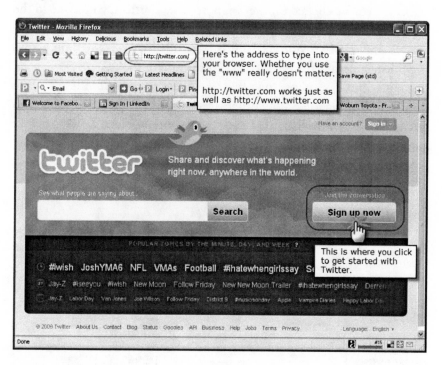

Keep this address in mind – Twitter.com. You can login from here, but more importantly it gives you instant access to the Search function on Twitter. It allows you to see what's happening without having to login to your account – just keep in mind that you can only make comments when you're signed in.

We won't go into too much detail right now. Just imagine you want to know what people are saying about your company. You type your company name into the box and click on the "Search" button.

The software searches every tweet for a mention of whatever you put into that box. When you search for your company name, you get to see all the things people – i.e. your customers, employees, friends and not-so-friendlies – are saying about you.

Okay. Let's get back to the profile.

By the way, I'm only going to use screenshots that show the whole browser window when you need to see the website address. The rest of the time, I'm just going to show the part of the screen where we're actually filling things in. It saves a little bit of space, and there are a lot of screenshots to come.

Once you've clicked on the "Sign up now" button, you come to the page where you create your Username and Password.

Naturally, when you get to this page all the spaces will be blank. I've filled in details for me so you can see how it looks.

My actual username on Twitter is theconradhall. I'll give you details for finding me on the other sites, too, when we get to them. I'm just using "mrconradhall" for the screenshots because I already have accounts with these sites. The only way I can go through the signup process is to create new accounts for each site.

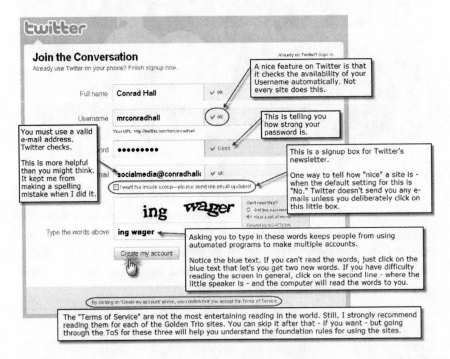

The next screen is where Twitter asks you to see if your friends are on Twitter. What it does is access your e-mail address book (for Gmail, Yahoo or AOL) and sees if the e-mail addresses there match any e-mail addresses on Twitter.

Every site has this step in the signup process. For now, I want you to skip it.

We'll come back and do this. It's just better for you to get your profile done – all the way done – and then connect with friends. Think of connecting with friends as having a house warming party. Which is better – to have the party while stuff is still in boxes (your profile is only partly filled in) or wait another day and have the place nicely decorated (your profile is complete)?

Right. I like the second option better, too. Since you're going to see the screen, let's take a quick look at it so you can see where the "skip this step" link is.

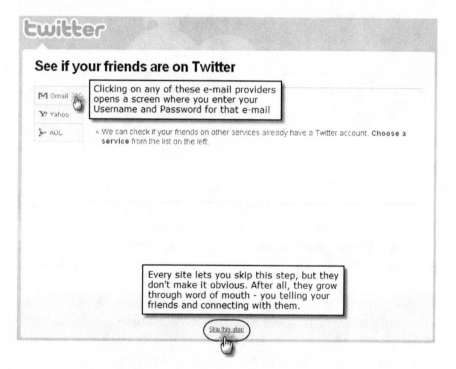

The next screen Twitter takes you to allows you to choose people to follow who are already on Twitter. If one of these people turns out to be one of your role models, then follow them. Otherwise, unselect all of them by clicking on the check mark next to "Select All."

When you follow someone, it means you want to know what he or she is doing. When we look at my Twitter home page in a second, you'll see that following someone means you get all his or her status updates.

If you follow everyone Twitter recommends, you're going to have a hard time finding the updates from the people you really do want to follow.

You can see the button in that last screenshot says "Finish." When you click on it, you're going to arrive at your home page. You know there's going to be a lot of stuff I want to cover on the home page and we'll definitely get to all of it. For right now, let's leave Twitter.

We've done what we came to do – create a profile. Now we're going to do the same thing for Facebook and LinkedIn. Once we've created a profile for each one, then we'll go back and fill in details. After we fill in details is when I'll cover the features on the home page for each site.

When you know what's on each home page, that's when we'll start putting things to use by connecting with a few people. So let's head over to Facebook and create a profile.

Facebook

Here's the landing page for Facebook:

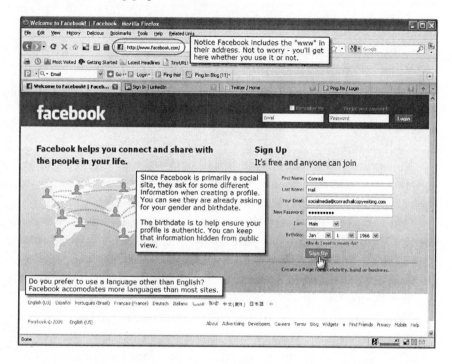

When you have filled in your information, just click on the "Sign Up" button. By the way, that's not my real birthday. I just put that in there for this example.

While we're here, let me mention something about passwords. First, you can change your password on any of these sites whenever you want. Some people say you should change your password monthly. Personally, I change mine once or twice a year.

One of the reasons I don't change the passwords more often is that I don't tell anyone what my passwords are. Well, that's not quite true. I tell my assistant and people working with me. But if I hire someone to do a specific project, then I change the password before they start and change it again when they're done.

When you set up your password, make sure you use at least three types of characters:

1. Numbers
2. Small case letters
3. Upper case letters (capitals)

Here's an example of a good password: uR2cuTe4mE

You want to make it memorable for yourself, but not something that's easy to figure out. Avoid using your name in the password just because some sites don't like your password to match anything in your profile.

What I do to get a good password is close my eyes and use my right index finger to hit the keyboard. Each time I touch the keyboard, I pull my hand back to my chest – it seems to make me more likely to hit a different spot on the keyboard. Here's an example of what I get:

l5hh52tynp

Make sure you have between 8 and 12 characters. I have 10 there, so now I pick two or three letters to make into capitals so the password looks like this: l5hH52TynP.

You can see right away that no one is going to figure this out easily. Of course, it's also not particularly memorable. My solution to that is to write my passwords down. I know, you're not supposed to do that, but I work from home and no one goes into my office except me and Yvette.

Do you remember how Twitter had text you had to type in (it's called Captcha text) to prove you're a human and not automated software? It's described in the screen capture on page 22. Facebook has the same thing only they put it on a separate page.

You'll see in the next screenshot that you can ask for different words or get an audio captcha text – just like in Twitter. Something Facebook has added for their site is a "Back" button. Just in case you want to double check that you put everything in correctly.

As with most sites, they give you links to the Terms of Service and their Privacy Policy. Twitter rolls theirs all up into one. (Mostly, I think, because there isn't any advertising on Twitter.) Facebook does have ads, as do most social media sites.

Here's the page with the captcha text:

If you happen to type in the wrong letters, the page just refreshes and shows you two new words.

When you've typed in the Captcha text, Facebook takes you to the page where you can find out if your friends are already on Facebook. You got it; this is where it's asking you to connect to your e-mail account. This is a step you want to skip for now. We can come back later to do this.

Here's the screen you'll see so you know where to find the "Skip this step" button:

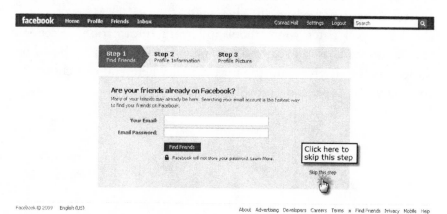

In Twitter you went to a screen where they recommended people you can follow. Facebook does the same sort of thing, but they use different criteria to increase the probability that you'll actually know the people they suggest.

The next screen for Facebook has two parts. The first part asks you to put in your high school, college or university and where you work.

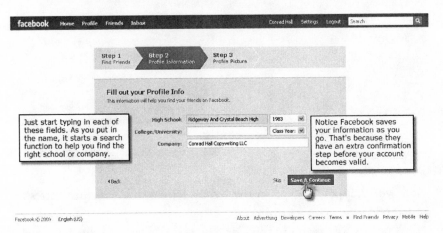

This is a good spot to mention that Facebook uses a second step to verify your account before making it active. That's part of why the system is saving the information you put in as you go.

Facebook sends you an e-mail to confirm your account – just like the double opt-in process many marketers use. You have to click on the confirmation link in the e-mail to finish activating your account. If you don't, Facebook will eventually close your account.

When you enter your school and work information, Facebook searches its database to see who has matching information. Based on those matches, it gives you the next screen where you can choose to connect with people you probably know.

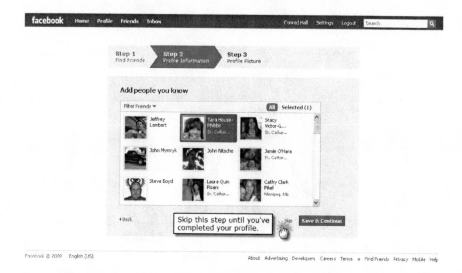

Definitely fill in the information about your schools and work. But when you get to this screen, click on the "Skip" link. Your information has already been saved as part of your profile so we'll be able to use it later to connect with these people.

Now you're going to add a photo to your profile. Facebook doesn't call them avatars because they specifically discourage people from using anything other than a real photo of themselves. The whole idea of Facebook is that you show who you are and make friends with new people.

The nice thing about this next screen is that it gives you two choices for putting a photo into your profile. Most sites just ask you to upload a photo from your computer. Facebook gives you the added option of taking a photo with your web cam.

Now, this isn't such a big deal when you're making your profile – it's just convenient if you don't have a personal photo on your computer. But once your profile is active, there might be lots of times when you want to take a photo and put it onto your profile right away. Being able to use a web cam to do it just makes things easier.

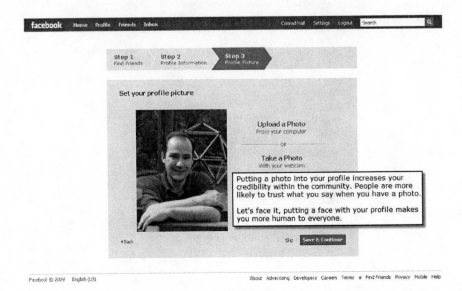

And that's it. You've completed the first stage of your Facebook profile.

When you click "Save & Continue" you're going to end up on your Facebook home page. It won't have much on it right now, but that's okay. We're going to move on to LinkedIn to create a profile there, then we're coming back to fill in all the details for each profile.

Before you know it, your profiles will be more complete than a lot of other users and you'll be making a terrific first impression with friends and strangers alike.

Here's what your home page will look like. Notice there are lots of links to help you connect with other people. We'll be back to do that shortly.

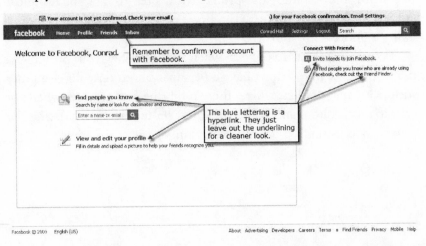

Now let's surf over to LinkedIn and create our last profile.

LinkedIn

Where Facebook is primarily a social site (Facebook has rules against using your personal profile for commercial gain), LinkedIn is a business networking site. They have their rules, too, they're just all centered on how you should do business instead of how to socialize.

There's one thing in particular to notice about the LinkedIn landing page. At the very bottom there is a line that says their terms and conditions "prohibit commercial use of this site."

This might seem like they're trying to keep you from advancing your business interests, but they aren't. What they don't want is someone putting a profile together and using it to sell something. You can tell people about what you do, invite them to your shop, even set up business deals on LinkedIn. What you can't do is turn LinkedIn into a storefront. It's a place for networking.

Here's the landing page for LinkedIn where you begin the sign up process:

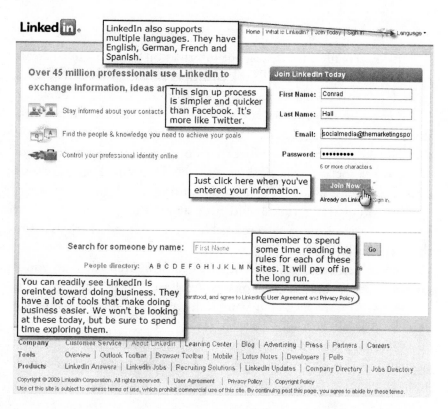

The sign up process for LinkedIn is very short. When you click on the "Join Now" button it takes you to a page where you fill in some basic information about your professional life. Here's what that page looks like:

This is actually the last page of information you'll fill in to create your LinkedIn account. We'll look at the pages that follow this in just a second, but first I'd like to review a note from the screenshot above.

There is an explanation circled with red in the screenshot above. Each field on this page has an explanation like that one. I think it's nice that LinkedIn is explaining what they do with the information. A lot of the other social media sites just ask the questions. Even Facebook doesn't give these kinds of explanations during their sign up process.

One other thing you should note about this page is that your current position is not a required field. There is no red asterisk next to that field name.

The reason for that is it doesn't really matter whether you're an employee or the business owner. All LinkedIn is trying to do is connect you with people in your industry and, where possible, in your local area.

When you've filled in the fields on this page, click on the "Continue" button and you go to a page that tells you to confirm your e-mail address. Here's what that page looks like:

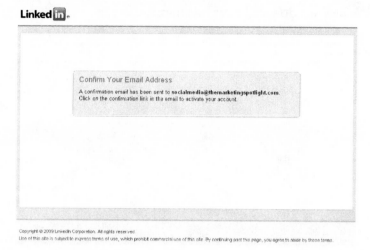

When you check your e-mail, you'll see this message:

LinkedIn

Click here to confirm your email address.

If the above link does not work, you can paste the following address into your browser:

https://www.linkedin.com/e/cnf/pAC8zHykO943RwuVKRFr8hydlrWyNgV7KYg8DhjdlAbyNN7TLRcBKHD/

You will be asked to log into your account to confirm this email address. Be sure to log in with your current primary email address.

We ask you to confirm your email address before sending invitations or requesting contacts at LinkedIn. You can have several email addresses, but one will need to be confirmed at all times to use the system.

If you have more than one email address, you can choose one to be your **primary email address**. This is the address you will log in with, and the address to which we will deliver all email messages regarding invitations and requests, and other system mail.

Thank you for using LinkedIn!

--The LinkedIn Team
http://www.linkedin.com/

When you click on the link in this e-mail it is going to open a new browser window. When you look at your browser, you're going to see two tabs for LinkedIn. One will have the screen from the screenshot above that tells you an e-mail is being sent to you.

The new window will have this message in it:

I'm sure this seems like a lot of extra work to confirm it's you asking for the account. The best way to view it is that LinkedIn takes your privacy – and their rules – quite seriously.

That's a very good way to view it because it happens to be true. Each of the Golden Trio sites takes the rules seriously. It's part of why they are successful.

When you click on the "Confirm" button on this screen, you go to the sign-in page for LinkedIn. At this point, your account has been created. If you wanted to, you could use LinkedIn with your profile just the way it is right now.

Obviously that's not a good idea. Before we move on, let me take a second to show you the sign-in page you'll go to:

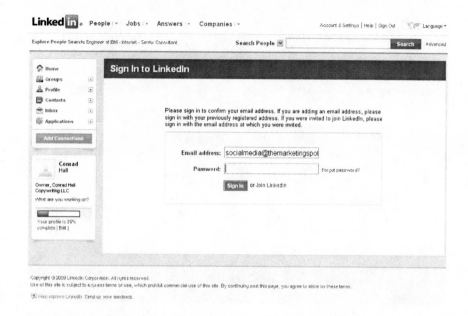

Once you type in your password and click "Sign In" your profile on LinkedIn is active.

That's why it takes you to a screen that continues building your profile.

At this point, we're going to finish off the profiles for each site. Since Twitter is very easy to complete, and LinkedIn is already taking you to a screen that builds your profile, we're going to work through the sites backward.

Let's finish your profile for LinkedIn, then we'll go back to Facebook and finish off with Twitter. Then we'll get connected with some people on each of the sites.

Let's start with the screen you'll see once you log in.

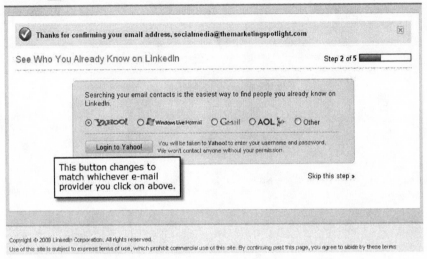

Just as we did with Facebook and Twitter, we're going to skip this step for now. When all the profiles are done, we'll come back through and connect with people from your e-mail address book.

You're probably thinking "We're here now, why don't we just do it now?"

That's a good question. You've already read the answer about making a good impression by having a completed profile when you connect with people, but there's another reason for doing it this way.

Right now, each of the sites is holding your hand to get you through this process. That works for them because their objective is to increase membership. It isn't so good for you because once you're inside the site, you aren't going to know how to do this on your own.

By skipping over this step now, it gives me the opportunity to show you how to do this process on your own inside the site. That means you can make new connections with people any time you want. It's that whole "Give a man a fish or teach a man to fish" sort of thing.

I prefer teaching people how to do it on their own. Once they know and understand, they're welcome to come back and hire me to do it for them. I just want to be sure they understand what's involved first.

That's why we're skipping this step until your profiles are complete.

When you click on "Skip this Step" on that screen, LinkedIn takes the information you put in about where you work and scans their database. They're looking for anyone who works for the same company, is in the same industry, or has a nearby zip code. In my case, since this is a second profile for me – I'm only making this profile so I can get all the screenshots we need – the only person it shows for me to connect with is me.

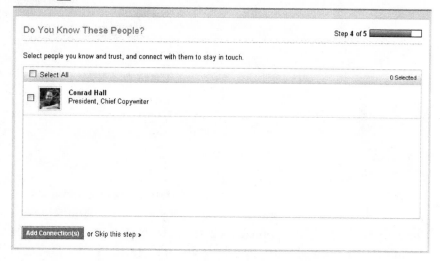

Would it be terribly narcissistic to connect with myself?

When you do this, you'll probably get quite a few recommendations on this screen. I had around four dozen when I created my real profile.

However, we're not ready to connect with anyone, so just click on "Skip this step" and we'll move on. You can see from the graphic in the upper right corner of the screen that we have one more step until LinkedIn says we've finished our profile.

The next screen LinkedIn sends you to is another opportunity to connect with people.

Here's what it looks like:

Linked in .

You're Almost Done   Step 5 of 5

Connect to more people you know and trust.
Enter email addresses of colleagues and friends to invite and connect.
Separate each address with a comma.

Add a personal message to your invitation ..

Send Invitations

Skip this step »

You know each of these sites is interested in increasing membership (the foundation of their business) when they ask you to connect with everyone in your address book, then try to hook you up with people already on the site and finish by asking you if there is anyone you know that might have been left out.

That's okay. Eventually you will connect with all those people; you're just doing it on your own terms. So click "Skip this step" and let's take a look at your profile.

Finishing Your Profiles

To this point, you might have been following along on the computer as we created your profiles. That's cool, and it's going to come in handy as we put the details into your profiles.

But there's something else I want you to do as we go through this section. Open a word processor (MSWord or something similar) and keep track of everything you put into your profiles. Let me explain why.

Part of this whole process of creating profiles is getting a document you can use any time you want it. The document is going to have all the information from your profiles on each of the Golden Trio sites. That way, when you join another site you can just open this document and copy & paste information into your new profile.

Aside from saving you some time when you join a new site, it also gives you one place where you keep track of all your profile updates. A profile update is different from a status update. Your status is what you're doing today or this afternoon. Your profile is a record of who you are and where you've been.

Keeping track of all your profile updates let's you see the progress you've made. Something a lot of folks haven't realized about social media yet is that it's an automatic journal. Status updates show the little steps you take each day toward a goal, and your profile updates show when you've achieved a goal.

Remember to look in Appendix D. The whole appendix is a note sheet you can use to get organized before you start, or make notes as you go.

Maybe you didn't realize this when you started reading – I certainly didn't realize it when I started with social media – but social media is an incredibly powerful, self-directed, self-improvement tool. Just watch and see if all those life coaches and career coaches out there don't clue in over the next two years to the fact that social media is a huge personal development tool.

Okay. Enough with the philosophy – we're here to get your profiles done and show you how to use social media to promote your business. Let's get back to LinkedIn.

LinkedIn

There is a ton of stuff on your LinkedIn home page. This isn't your profile; it's your home page for the LinkedIn site.

It gives you access to your profile, and everything else you can do on LinkedIn.

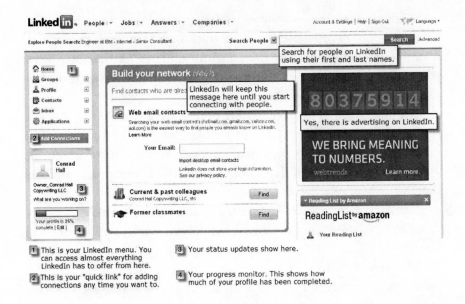

1. This is your LinkedIn menu. You can access almost everything LinkedIn has to offer from here.

3. Your status updates show here.

2. This is your "quick link" for adding connections any time you want to.

4. Your progress monitor. This shows how much of your profile has been completed.

All we're interested in for right now is item #4 – your progress monitor. We're going to finish your profile.

When you click on the "Edit" link you go to your Profile page. Just so you know, you can also get to your Profile page by clicking on "Profile" in the menu (#1 in the screenshot above).

The fastest way to complete your profile is to import your resume. LinkedIn offers that option on the right side of your profile page. It's still going to take some editing to finish, but it will get a lot of the information into your profile in a hurry.

Since you're going to have to do some editing anyway, I'll let you experiment with importing your resume (it's very easy), and focus on making sure you know what the parts of your profile look like and how they work.

Let's start with the top of your profile page.

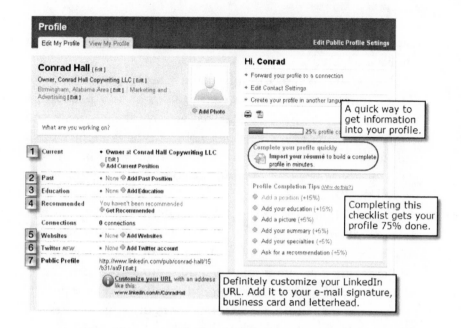

LinkedIn does everything they can to encourage you to complete your profile. They let you import your resume, there's a checklist on the right side of the page that gets your profile three quarters done in a hurry, and they put the progress monitor on both sides of the page.

You definitely get the idea that a completed profile is valuable.

We're gong to zero in on the parts numbered 1 through 7.

1. Current position
2. Past positions
3. Education
4. Recommendations
5. Websites
6. Twitter Connection
7. Public Profile URL

When we're done with these, we'll move farther down the page.

1. Current Position

All LinkedIn has for this position is the information you put in while creating your profile. You still need to add when you started your current position, and a description of what it is you do.

Click on "Edit" just under your current position and you'll go to a screen where you can choose which year you started, and enter a description of what you do. Just like a resume, be sure to emphasize accomplishments over actions. You want to show what you have achieved.

And be sure to copy this information into the word processor file you started to keep track of your profiles, or use Appendix D. When I set up my profiles, I looked at each of the screens and made a few notes. Then I went away from the computer to sit and think about what I wanted to write. After I was happy with what I had written, I returned to the computer and put answers into all the fields.

You can do it either way – fill in the blanks as we go, or take time to write it all down and come back later – just as long as you keep track of everything in a file. It will pay off in the long run.

Notice there is also a link to "Add Current Position." That's because LinkedIn allows you to have more than one. This is especially handy for entrepreneurs who operate more than one business, or who are working a day job while they get off the ground.

2. Past Position

There's no limit on how many past positions you can put into your profile.

The information for a past position is the same as your current position, only LinkedIn doesn't have any information to start with. So instead of starting with the company name and your title filled in, you have to put something into every field.

There's also a small difference with the date function. Obviously a current position is from one date to the present. With a past position, you indicate the month and year when you started and the month and year when you finished.

There's also a second place where you can enter your work experience.

Scroll down the profile page until you come to the "Experience" heading. It looks like this:

Experience   ✚ Add Position

Owner at **Conrad Hall Copywriting LLC** [Edit]

Marketing and Advertising industry
Currently holds this position Please tell us when you started in this position!

You can provide a brief description for this position.

No recommendations for this position [Request Recommendations]

This image is taken from the profile I set up for writing this chapter – that's why there is only one position shown.

After your profile is completed, this is where you'll go to enter a new position or edit any of your experience information. Just click on "Add Position" to add new information or look beside a particular position and click "Edit" to change the information.

3. Education

Education also has a second area for entering information. It follows immediately after the area for entering experience.

It's a little more involved when you add education information. LinkedIn wants to know what country and province/state the school was in, what degree/diploma you obtained, and your field of study.

Interestingly, there are two areas where you can enter descriptive information. One is for any activities or societies you participated with. This is easy to understand.

The other area is for "Additional Notes." This is where you put things you did while you were at school, but that weren't part of your academic studies.

For example, being in a play, club or sports team would go in the area for activities and societies. Being part of a school radio station, coordinating community activities and other off-campus pursuits all go under Additional Notes.

Remember to keep adding all this information to your profile file or Appendix D. As your business grows, you're going to end up having an assistant look after updating your profile. When that happens, you're going to be glad you took the time to put everything into one spot.

Social media is growing and changing. When I ran through the site list for *friends, followers and Customer Evangelists*, there were more than 100 sites from the previous year that no longer existed.

You can bet there will be new sites that come along and you're going to join them. It will be much easier to have someone do the work of creating a profile if you're keeping everything in one place.

Your profile is also your brand. It helps other people to recognize you when you can keep the same username on every site, the same (or similar) photo, and the same basic information. We all hate routine – until we're trying to find someone. Then we're grateful for consistency.

4. Recommendations

There are two ways to get recommended.

The most common is to contact someone you know and ask them to recommend you. Naturally, they are going to recommend you based on the work you've done together. They pick what position you held when you worked together, and they write a recommendation.

The other way is to find a position in your profile you want a recommendation for. Then you look for people who can give you the recommendation you want. To do it this way, just look at the last line in any entry for Experience or Education.

The last line tells you how many recommendations you have for that position. In brackets is [Request Recommendation]. Just click on that link and find people to give you a recommendation.

5. Websites

Naturally you want to include the URL for any website you have – your blog, business site, even a landing page if you want to.

You only get to list three sites, so list your best ones first. And I do recommend you avoid listing a landing page unless you have no other options.

Interestingly, this is also where you enter your interests & hobbies, groups & associations you belong to, and any honors or awards you have received.

6. Twitter Connection

This is an excellent example of how things are changing in social media. Twitter and LinkedIn weren't connected when I originally wrote this chapter.

This feature allows you to connect your Twitter account to LinkedIn so your tweets show up as status updates in your profile.

If, like me, you use a social media aggregator (I use Ping.fm) to post your status updates, then you want to be careful about making this connection. You can see how updating Twitter and LinkedIn through Ping, AND having Twitter connected to LinkedIn, is going to give you duplicate entries on LinkedIn.

There's a quick fix for this.

When you make the connection, it gives you a choice between including all your tweets and just including tweets with the #in hashtag. Be sure to choose that second option.

This connects the two services, and you can keep using your aggregator without creating duplicate entries in LinkedIn.

7. Public Profile URL

I heartily recommend getting a LinkedIn custom URL that uses your name if at all possible.

It definitely makes the URL easier to remember, and it makes a better impression than the standard URL LinkedIn provides.

You can find my LinkedIn profile at http://www.linkedin.com/in/theconradhall.

There are two more items that come right after the line for Public Profile. They are your Summary and your Specialties. Here's where to find them:

Think of your summary as an elevator speech. You want just a couple of paragraphs to show readers what it is you do.

Being able to add your specialties is a bonus. It means you can put a little more into your summary.

A quirk of LinkedIn is that it recognizes different paragraphs in the Summary but not in Specialties. So, even if you try to separate your specialties into different paragraphs, LinkedIn is just going to run them together as a single paragraph. (Hopefully they'll change that soon.)

The last two items for your LinkedIn profile are Personal Information and Contact Settings. These are both at the bottom of the profile page.

Personal Information [Edit]

Phone:	561-623-9441 (work)
Address:	5204 Bessemer Super Hwy. Brighton, AL 353020 U.S.A.
	410-250 Cassandra Blvd. Toronto, ON M3A 1V1 Canada
IM:	Add an IM to your profile.
Birthday:	1966
Marital status:	Single

Contact Settings [Edit]

Please be prepared to help me understand your business and your target customers. What is unique about the product and service you offer? You are welcome to ask questions about Direct Response Marketing and how it can benefit your business.

Interested In:

- consulting offers
- expertise requests
- reference requests
- new ventures
- business deals
- getting back in touch

When you click "Edit" next to personal settings, you'll see there is a little more information you can enter than what shows in my LinkedIn profile. That's because I've chosen to keep some information private.

While you're filling in your profile, watch for the image of a lock beside each entry. If there is a lock, then you can set the privacy level for that specific information. For example, you can put your birthday into LinkedIn and set your profile so that it shows only for people in your network.

Your contact settings show people what it is you're looking to get from LinkedIn.

It's always a good idea to look at this part of someone's profile before you contact them. You might not get far contacting someone about a joint venture if their profile doesn't indicate that is of interest to them.

Your profile is complete, and you're ready to connect with people. Next we'll finish your Facebook and Twitter profiles, then walk through how to connect with people. I'll show you how to do it through Twitter because once you know how to do it on one site, all the others are the same. Of course, I'll make a point of showing you where to go on Facebook and LinkedIn to get started.

There are still lots of features for you to explore on LinkedIn. Be sure to set aside time each week to explore the Golden Trio sites. After all, trying to cover everything you can do on these sites is enough material for several books. (Hmmm…that gives me some new book ideas…)

Facebook

Compared to LinkedIn, Facebook is going to seem like a cakewalk.

It isn't that the Facebook system is any easier to use, it's just that people always seem to shy away form describing themselves positively when it comes to their work. Because Facebook is all about recreation and being social, my clients seem to have an easier time with this profile.

My advice to everyone is the same: Blow your own horn. If you don't, no one else will.

Think of it this way – you're just telling the truth. That it happens to show you in a good light is a bonus. That you put some effort into choosing the best wording for your profile is wise.

Your Facebook profile has 4 areas for you to put information into:
1. Basic Information
2. Personal Information
3. Contact Information
4. Education and Work

Instead of walking you through each area, I decided the best way to show you this profile is to give you a copy of mine. It's in Appendix E.

This is also a good way to show you what I mean by keeping all your profile information in one place. It's especially helpful to me because I keep a list of the sites I belong to with my profile information.

Whenever anything changes in my profile, I have a ready list of the places that need to be updated.

Even though I'm not going to run through every screen for your Facebook profile, there are some pointers I want to share. The first one relates to two things in your Basic Information.

Facebook gives you space to express your political and religious views. It isn't a lot of space, but it's there. My advice is that you be moderate in what you write.

You're here for business. Religion and politics are topics that often cause disagreement. No matter what you put in those fields – even if you leave them blank – you're going to offend someone. Since my business doesn't involve religion or politics, my practice is to keep my views to myself.

You'll see what I mean when you read my Facebook profile in the appendix.

The area for personal information is all about things you like to do. When you put information into this area, give people some detail. This is where you get to make a personal impression so be personable.

Interestingly, Facebook makes all the information in the personal fields (except Favorite Quotations and About Me) into hyperlinks. What the system does is treat each sentence as a keyword phrase. If someone clicks on a sentence, Facebook looks for any information in its own database that matches that phrase.

Look in Appendix E to see how I've arranged my information. I use just one or two keywords then put in a comma. (The comma is what Facebook uses to separate keywords.) After the comma comes the personal information about why I like whatever I've listed.

When you edit your contact information you'll see the lock icon again. Pay attention to these and use them to protect your privacy.

It's also in this area that you'll see a link to create a Facebook badge for your website. What this means is it gives you a piece of code you can have put on your website so people can click on it and go to your Facebook profile. This is a particularly good thing to have if your business is improved by people liking you. Being able to go to your Facebook profile can help them do just that.

The area for education and work information is similar to what you put into your LinkedIn profile. Facebook does give you space for putting more than one position, high school and/or college/university. There's a link for each one that says "Add Another…"

When you're finished entering your work and education information, your profile is complete. You're ready to connect with other people.

So let's take a quick look at Twitter. Finishing your profile here takes about 4 seconds (sort of) and then we're on to making some connections.

Twitter

There are just three spots for you to go when finishing your Twitter profile, and all of them are under Settings.

When you click on Settings in the menu at the top of the screen, the page you land on is for your Account. Let's take a look at that so you can see how the page is set up. The image for this is large – a whole page – so it's on the next page. (This image is taken from the account I set up for writing the guide – that's why so many of the fields are blank.)

Notice there are tabs across the top of the page. That's what we're going to use to find the other two spots you need to visit.

First, let's look at your account settings.

Twitter automatically puts in your name, username, email and time zone. It leaves you 5 areas to customize.

The first one is your URL. You can put your blog, business website or any other URL in here.

Then comes your One Line Bio. This is important because it shows on your profile and it's all people get to know about you other than what you put in your tweets. Since you have a limit of 160 characters, take a little bit of time to work out what you want to say.

The line for location is basically whatever city you're in. If you travel a lot, feel free to change that as often as you like.

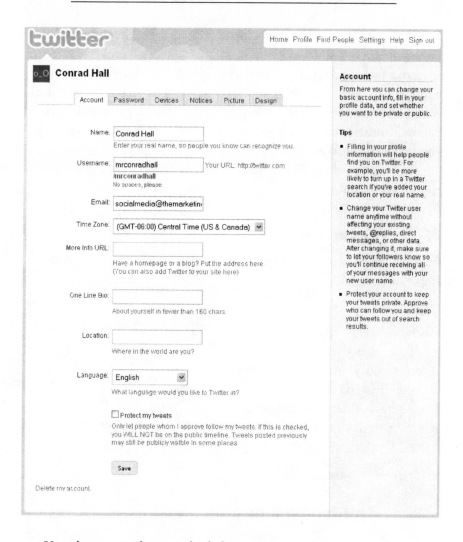

You do get to choose which language you want to use, but your choices are limited to either English or Japanese.

The last item allows you to make your tweets private. If you do this, no one will be able to see your tweets unless you approve them as a follower. This might be a good thing to do if you're using Twitter as an online journal. But since you're reading this book, my guess is you want to use Twitter to further your business interests.

In that case, definitely keep your tweets public.

From here you can click on the tab for Picture. Adding a photo to Twitter is the same as adding one to Facebook or LinkedIn. Just find the file on your computer and click "Upload Photo."

The last place to visit is Notices. This is where you control how often you get e-mail from Twitter.

I recommend keeping all of the options checked until you are more comfortable with Twitter. If you start to use a service like Tweetdeck, then you can remove some notifications. For now, keeping them checked means you don't have to log in to your account every day – you can just check your e-mail.

And guess what? Your profiles are complete. Now it's time to connect with some people.

Making Connections

First, let's make sure you know where to go for each of the Golden Trio sites.

Twitter

Click on "following."

That takes you to a screen that informs you you're not following anyone. Imagine that.

Right beside that statement is a link that says "add or invite more." Click on that link.

Clicking on this link takes you to the page we saw in the screenshot on page 28.

This is where you're going to access your e-mail account to import the names of people you can connect with.

From here on, the process is the same for almost every social media site. That means we can walk through it once, and you're good to go.

The first thing you do is choose which e-mail provider you're using. In the case of Twitter, they only offer Gmail, Yahoo and AOL. Other sites (such as Facebook) can import contacts from just about anywhere. One place they can't import contacts from is your domain mail.

For example, Facebook can't import contacts from conrad@ theconradhall.com. To bring my contacts in from there requires me to export the contacts into a CSV (comma separated values) file and then upload that file to Facebook.

No need to worry if you don't know what that means. If you have a domain e-mail – one that uses the name of your website – you probably also have a webmaster. Just tell her what you want to do and she'll get it done for you.

After you choose your e-mail provider, simply type in your username and password. The site will import your contacts and compare it to the members. Here's what it looks like:

Find people. Follow them.

| | Find on Twitter | Find on other networks | Suggested Users |

M Gmail

Y Yahoo   Your Email   [   ]   🔒 Email Security
                                                          We don't store your login,
Y AOL   your password is
                         Email Password [   ]   submitted securely, and
                                                          we don't email without
                                                          your permission.

Continue

After you enter the username and password for your e-mail account, just click "Continue."

The site will start by showing you the people from your e-mail account who are already using the site. This gives you a chance to connect with people you know. It's like walking into a party and looking for your friends.

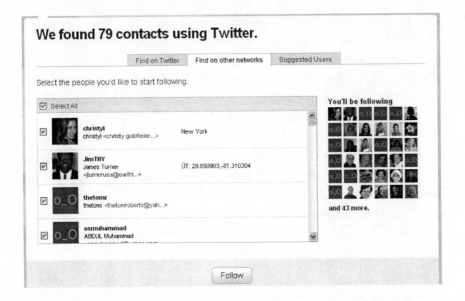

Choose which people you want to connect with by putting or removing a check mark next to their name. The default setting for most sites is that you want to connect with everyone.

When you click "Continue," or in the case of Twitter "Follow," the next screen shows you people from your address book who aren't on the site. Naturally, this is an opportunity for you to invite them to join you on the site.

When you click the continue button on other sites, they generally send a message to the person asking them to confirm you as a friend or associate before actually connecting you. This helps to maintain privacy on the sites.

It also gives you a chance to personalize the message a little. Not every site lets you personalize the message, so take advantage of the opportunity when you have it. For people you know well, you may even want to invite them individually rather than as part of a big group just so you can personalize the message for them.

When you get to the page where you have an opportunity to invite others to the site, take a minute to think that situation through. The typical default setting is for no one to be selected – you have to go through the list and deliberately put a check mark next to each person's name who you want to invite.

This is because you want to avoid inviting people at their work e-mail address, and there may be one or two people you know who simply don't want this kind of invitation. Social media sites are all about being polite and considerate toward others, so don't just send a blanket invitation to everyone in your address book.

A lot of sites let you customize this invitation, too. If you have that option, use it.

Now that you're finished with your address book, the site probably has a few people it will suggest as possible connections for you. It may be based on having attended the same school, working at the same company, or living in the same city. Take a minute to look through the list and see if there is anyone you want to connect with.

Okay. You've created your profiles, filled in the details and connected with some people. Now it's time to connect with a few role models.

Every site offers the ability to search its members. Just type in the name of a role model and click the "search" button. Often, this results in several people showing up. When that happens, just look through the list to see if the right person is there. If they aren't, then maybe that person is not using the site you're on.

Of course, if they are there, then you should try to connect with them.

My recommendation is that you choose no more than 6 role models to connect with in the beginning. You have three sites to explore, connecting with 6 role models on each – even if they're the same six people every time – is going to keep you busy while you explore the sites. Wait until you're comfortable using the sites before trying to pay attention to the actions of a lot of role models.

And that brings us to the end of creating your profiles.

There's still a lot for you to explore on the Golden Trio sites. If you'd like help doing it, you're welcome to contact me at conrad@ theconradhall.com. I offer both group and individual sessions to help business owners get up and running with social media.

There's also a great book written by a friend of mine – Jim Turner. The title is *Social Networking – The 21st Century Way to Find New Clients.*

Jim uses social media exclusively for getting clients, and he knows the Golden Trio inside and out. Rather than try to duplicate what Jim has done, I'll suggest you get a copy of his book. Just go to www. awaionline.com/soc/hach to get your copy today.

Jim walks you through every aspect of using social media to promote yourself and your business. The one thing that's lacking is step-by-step instructions for setting up profiles – that's why I included this chapter. When you put *friends, followers and Customer Evangelists* together with Jim's book, you have a winning combination.

To get you started in making connections, here are the URLs (universal resource locators or web addresses) for my social media profiles:

http://facebook.com/theconradhall

http://www.linkedin.com/in/theconradhall

http://twitter.com/theconradhall

You can follow everything I do (almost) through FriendFeed. When you're finished with setting up profiles on the Golden Trio, FriendFeed should be your next stop. For starters, it's owned by Facebook so you know it's going to be around for a long time.

The best feature of FriendFeed is that it gives anyone who wants to follow you a single location where they can see everything you're doing on 58 other sites (and they're adding more sites all the time). Here's the URL for my FriendFeed profile:

http://friendfeed.com/theconradhall

One thing you won't find on FriendFeed are my articles. I write for Technorati and Blog Critics, and am an Expert Author with EzineArticles.com.

http://technorati.com/people/technorati/theconradhall

http://blogcritics.org/writers/theconradhall

http://www.ezinearticles.com/?expert=Conrad_Hall

Take a second to connect with me now, and subscribe to the RSS feed from my blog, The Marketing Spotlight:

http://themarketingsporlight.com/?feed=rss

Now on to see the social networking sites.

4. The Social Networking Sites

Site	Google	Alexa	Compete
http://www.facebook.com	9	4	3

It's a nice place to break free of the isolation every home-based business owner feels. You can easily get lost in reading updates and replying, so be sure you only login when your work is done for the day!

Facebook is a much more social place than it is business. For me, it's a great place to put up the photos I take when traveling. Photography is something I enjoy, and Facebook gives me a place to share it.

Sharing things you do as a hobby also adds depth to your online presence. That added dimension is something that will work in your favor to draw prospects to you.

http://www.MySpace.com	9	11	10

This is a popular site most people are probably familiar with. For those who aren't, MySpace.com allows you to find/make friends, post photos, videos, and music, and it even allows you to choose a URL for your MySpace account.

Here's an interesting note: MySpace.com is one of two social sites I belong to where I get messages from, supposedly, attractive women who want to have a serious, meaningful relationship – based entirely on "reading" my profile. Either I write a great profile (for two sites, at least) or they need to do a better job of dumping spammers.

http://www.twitter.com	9	31	46

Twitter is all the rage in social media. I use it, but I don't think it's as powerful as Facebook or LinkedIn.

Within the limit of 140 characters, Twitter is an unparalleled tool for staying in touch with the world. People who like my books and blog posts follow me on Twitter. Even folks who see my tweets, and like them, decide to follow me.

My only reason for saying it isn't as powerful as Facebook or LinkedIn is that 140 character limit. Maybe I just like the look of my own typing a little too much. ;-)

Site	Google	Alexa	Compete
http://my.opera.com/community/	9	712	3459

Opera is a browser – not the musical where the "fat lady" sings.

Opera's community is a blog and photo sharing site for users. It has the same "feel" as MySpace or Facebook as far as having a mailbox and connecting with friends. Opera gives you 1GB of free space for your blog, and there are (just like WordPress) lots of widgets you can add to your blog.

http://www.slashdot.org	9	1899	93,892

Slashdot's own tagline is: "News for nerds. Stuff that matters."

You'll find news items, book reviews, gaming updates, and more. This is definitely not LinkedIn or Facebook. Slashdot impresses me as a well targeted, focused site with both free and membership options.

A note about the membership option: It doesn't give you access to "extra" information. It gives you access to the site without advertising.

http://www.livejournal.com	8	93	321

When you use this for yourself, think of it as an online diary. You can also use it to interact with communities of people who share one of your interests.

A cool element of the site for personal users is being able to set the privacy level for everything you post. When you put something into your journal you want to keep strictly private – just set the privacy level to private for that post.

Site	Google	Alexa	Compete
http://www.orkut.com	8	121	4124

Orkut is operated by Google – one more free service from the search engine giant.

My experience with Orkut isn't extensive, but there is one thing I definitely do NOT like. When you invite friends to join your network, Orkut only sends an auto-invite which is less personal. You can't modify the invitation it sends – and you don't even get to see it before the invitation is sent.

http://www.ning.com	8	155	207

Ning.com is free. It allows you to set up your own social network with an appearance that is very much like a WordPress blog. Visit jimturnersmm.ning.com to see a good example of a Ning.com social network in action.

http://www.linkedin.com	8	91	82

This is the only site I know of specifically designed for B2B (business to business) networking.

LinkedIn allows you to fill in extensive information about you and your business. You can make introductions to other people through your network of immediate contacts and give (or receive) recommendations for high quality work.

http://www.last.fm	8	316	603

Last.fm recommends music, videos, and concerts based on what you listen to. This site is particularly focused on helping musicians and label owners promote their work.

You can make comments on the music, share your interests with other listeners, and find listeners who share your interests.

Site	Google	Alexa	Compete
http://www.pandora.com	8	451	338

Pandora is part of the Music Genome Project. Their objective is to provide an analysis of all the music available from the last century.

That might sound a little dull – but don't be deceived. It allows you to put the name of any artist or song into Pandora's search function and find other songs and artists that are similar from a musical point of view. It's a great way to discover new music.

The social aspect is sharing your musical interests with other users.

WARNING: Pandora has introduced a limit on free users. You are allowed only 40 hours of free listening per month. After that, you either wait until next month or purchase a subscription.

Site	Google	Alexa	Compete
http://www.secondlife.com	8	3621	7389

Secondlife.com is a virtual world designed by its users. It requires you to download the SecondLife Viewer and install it on your computer.

You must be 18 years of age or older to join SecondLife.com.

Without question, SecondLife.com is the most complex social media site I have discovered. There is a free membership level and a host of paid membership levels. The primary use of SecondLife.com seems to be corporate training.

Site	Google	Alexa	Compete
http://home.spaces.live.com	7	5	4

Provided by Microsoft, this site allows you to set up a blog, post videos, and make use of other modules and gadgets.

Site	Google	Alexa	Compete
http://www.hi5.com	7	32	506

Based in San Francisco, CA, hi5.com is similar in structure and function to Facebook or MySpace. It has added functionality that allows you to use "hi5 coins." In addition to friends and photos, it also allows you to flirt, make a scrapbook, and keep a journal.

Site	Google	Alexa	Compete
http://www.friendster.com	7	73	1526

Friendster is for adults 18 and older.

Friendster allows you to build a blog, play games, post photos and videos, find your friends, and lets you review the posts, photos and videos of others as well.

http://www.fotolog.com	7	161	6775

Specifically for photographers.

Two account levels: Basic and Gold. Basic allows you to upload only one photo per day. Gold allows you to upload 6 photos per day.

http://www.bebo.com	7	165	406

Provided by AOL.

Allows you to connect to Facebook, MySpace, YouTube, Delicious, Twitter, AIM, AOL Mail, Google Mail, Yahoo! Mail updates, and your cell phone.

http://www.yelp.com	7	399	35

Yelp is focused on the U.S. to help users find great local businesses like dentists, hair stylists, and mechanics.

There are 26 city editions of Yelp (e.g. Chicago, San Francisco, and Honolulu).

Yelp is available in the UK.

http://www.squidoo.com	7	483	N/A

Founded by Seth Godin.

The stated function of the site is to make it easy for people to create free pages (called "lenses") on topics in which they are interested, and to earn royalties for their good content. Nearly 40% of all Squidoo users donate the royalties they earn from the site to charity. (Taken directly from the site.)

Looking for a place to build your platform and be recognized as an expert? This is a good place to do it.

Site	Google	Alexa	Compete
http://www.xanga.com	7	492	1152

This is a blogging community.

http://www.classmates.com	7	546	61

Specifically for re-connecting with your classmates.
It covers Canada, U.S., Austria, France, Germany, and Sweden.

http://www.myyearbook.com	7	552	129

Founded by Dave and Catherine – brother and sister – a high school senior and a junior.

The site started with a high-school/college focus. It is now growing to encompass much more than just schools. They have also attracted an interesting array of talent to their Board of Directors.

http://www.meetup.com	7	1,093	631

This appears to be a "local service" at first, but there's more to it. You can create a Meetup Group in your town based on your interest – whether it's hiking, entrepreneurship, or kite flying – and arrange meetings with people who join your group. You can also use it to find groups in other locations.

Going on vacation and want to meet people with similar interests? This is a site that can help you do it.

http://www.mybloglog.com	7	1945	0

This is a Yahoo service. It is a blogging community.

http://www.care2.com	7	3099	N/A

Targeting healthy and green living.

Site	Google	Alexa	Compete
http://www.43things.com	7	3588	1975

The foundation for the book *Dream It! List It! Do It!*
A site for setting and achieving goals – and discovering who you are along the way.

http://www.tribe.net	7	5382	2800

Tribe.net has a local focus. They help you to connect with people in your city.

http://www.librarything.com	7	6481	3345

The ultimate site for book lovers.
You can list all your books online and create a catalogue for yourself (and keep it entirely private – if you want to). Then you can share your books, opinions, and reading list with other bibliophiles.

http://www.couchsurfing.com	7	12,734	38,080

Take the name literally. This site allows you to arrange to "surf" on other people's couches and play host to other "couchsurfers." Instead of staying in a hotel, you make friends and stay on someone's couch – or they stay on yours.

CouchSurfing International is a non-profit organization with members around the globe. They have an extensive verification process and provide a self-moderating community (think Neighborhood Watch).

It's also free to join. You might just have some of the best travel experiences of your life.

http://www.ryze.com	7	19,733	45,990

Specifically a business networking site.

Site	Google	Alexa	Compete
http://www.takingitglobal.org	7	704,023	921,758

Targeting youth interested in global issues and creating positive change.

http://www.consumating.com	7	17,561,525	998,220

Recently re-named to www.help.com. This is a service provided by CNET.com.

This is a network of people dedicated to helping you. You can join to get questions answered, or to be available to answer questions.

http://www.hubpages.com	6	352	300

Similar to Squidoo.com. This is an online publishing community that enables you to produce Hubs (content-rich web pages) on subjects you know and enjoy.

http://www.buzznet.com	6	793	883

An online community to share music news, videos, comments, and more.

http://www.gaiaonline.com	6	832	1710

A virtual world for teens. It has its own economy, chat forums, art contests, and Gaia cinemas for watching movies online.

http://www.imvu.com	6	994	1352

This site is still in the BETA stage. It requires a download to your computer.

It provides an animated 3D chat experience.

Site	Google	Alexa	Compete
http://www.blackplanet.com	6	1395	1238

This is the "largest Black community online." It is a free service for networking.

http://www.piczo.com	6	1514	5036

Targeting teens worldwide to creatively express themselves, build personal communities, and share experiences with their friends in a safe environment.

http://www.mog.com	6	3969	3687

This site targets music lovers and is dedicated to helping you find the most up-to-date information about your favorite artist or group.

http://www.ecademy.com	6	6808	24,300

A business networking site founded in 1998.

I know several people who are members and they are enjoying good results. It's a combination of Meetup.com and LinkedIn.com

http://www.reunion.com	6	7187	104

Recently re-named to www.mylife.com.

This site targets social relationships. It searches several other networking sites to connect you with people on a social level. It is specifically NOT a business networking site.

http://www.gather.com	6	8303	6115

The focus here is on meeting new people socially. Rather than trying to connect with people from your past, gather.com invites you to meet new people and discover new interests.

Site	Google	Alexa	Compete
http://www.migente.com	6	8911	6873

Run by the same company operating www.blackplanet.com.
This is a social networking site for Latinos.

http://www.travbuddy.com	6	11,829	11,545

Targeting travelers. This site helps you to connect with travel partners, share photos, and post reviews of places you have visited.
If you're into travel, this is a site you need to explore.
Must be 18 years of age.

http://www.dogster.com	6	14,704	3752

Targeted to dog owners.

http://www.eons.com	6	19,002	7660

An online community for Boomers.

http://www.fanpop.com	5	1259	1207

Fanpop is a network of fan clubs for fans of television, movies, music, and more to discuss and share photos, videos, news, and opinions with fellow fans.

http://www.wayn.com	5	2031	9175

A lifestyle and travel social network.

http://www.downelink.com	5	8796	16,872

An online community for the LBGTQ community.

Site	Google	Alexa	Compete
http://www.nexopia.com	5	14,490	57,030

Canadian youth-oriented social networking site.

| http://www.faceparty.com | 5 | 19,309 | 160,353 |

A paid, British networking site. Cost = £25 (that's $41.37 USD on 15 Aug 09 – exchange rates fluctuate).

There is a significant amount of vulgarity and profanity used. Not everyone's cup of tea, but a good site if it catches your interest.

| http://www.blurty.com | 5 | 64,369 | 79,428 |

A site for creating your own blog. Must be 18 years of age.

| http://www.musicforte.com | 5 | 80,046 | 39,854 |

Targeting the Indie Music Community.

A unique feature is their catalog of sheet music (more than 300,000 choices).

| http://www.tagworld.com | 5 | 116,681 | 141,113 |

A social networking community.

The unique aspect of this site is how little it communicates about itself. There is no "About" page, or anything to tell you what the site is trying to do.

| http://www.deadjournal.com | 5 | 171,880 | 132,900 |

A place for angry people to post their rants.

Remember, everything on the internet is _on the internet_. Anyone can find it.

Site	Google	Alexa	Compete
http://www.tripconnect.com	5	481,037	228,865

A travel networking site. This is similar to www.travbuddy.com. Combine both sites for best effect.

http://www.zaadz.com	5	716,007	281,782

Recently re-named to www.Gaia.com.
A social networking community for the eco-conscious.

http://www.unyk.com	4	4688	23,318

An online address book.
When you join, you ask your contacts to join. Anytime a contact changes their information, you are automatically updated.

http://www.yuwie.com	4	9333	22,883

A social networking site where you create a blog and get paid each time someone views your pages.

http://www.mobango.com	4	9334	50,566

This site is in BETA.
Download free applications for your cell phone.

http://www.mygamma.com	4	60,337	727,907

Social networking on your cell phone. Strictly non-commercial.

http://www.xuqa.com	4	73,563	N/A

A game site.

Site	Google	Alexa	Compete
http://www.graduates.com	4	101,141	104,317

A site for connecting with former schoolmates.

http://www.decayenne.com	4	128,139	476,663

You must apply to become a member of this community.
"At Decayenne we appreciate intellectual diversity and leadership; we encourage discussions and hold up humanistic values. In this liberal environment, we rely on responsible, high minded interaction between members in order to maintain our cherished civility."

http://www.meetin.org	4	173,737	73,177

A social networking site for meeting people locally. It is similar to www.meetup.com.

http://www.trade-pals.com	4	238,322	448,744

A B2B directory of professionals with two membership levels: Basic and Professional.

http://www.listography.com	4	315,421	188,772

A personal tool for creating a database of lists that you also share on the internet.

http://www.profileheaven.com	4	545,032	1,102,259

A site for young people to meet.

http://www.wallop.com	4	926,018	4,359,466

Provides two applications (featured on Facebook and Bebo) that let you tell people you care and plan events.

Site	Google	Alexa	Compete
http://www.passado.com	4	1,207,411	2,043,408

Re-named to http://uk.wasabi.com. A site for re-connecting with classmates.

http://www.gazzag.com	4	2,163,303	0

Re-named to Octopop (http://en.octopop.com/gazzag_users.jsp). This site is similar to Facebook.

http://www.directmatches.com	3	17,586	22,784
http://www.dandelife.com	3	272,206	215,210
http://www.refernet.net	3	2,692,948	2,034,709
http://uk.tribe.net	2	5381	2800
http://www.flingr.com	2	257,893	984,797
http://www.yapperz.com	2	1,404,982	3,811,359
http://www.refer-online.com	2	2,694,981	0
http://www.mylocalspot.com	1	4,234,791	0
http://community.adlandpro.com	0	15,781	0

Before finishing this chapter, there are two other sites I want to mention. Both are from Google, and one is available while the other is in Beta (being developed).

The sites are:
1. Google Friend Connect, and
2. Gwave

Google Friend Connect

The idea behind Google Friend Connect (GFC) is that it will "instantly" make your site into a social media venue. By adding one or more of their gadgets, you give visitors to your site the ability to sign in, leave comments, rate content, and participate in polls.

GFC does everything it claims to do, and will add a social media dimension to your site. But I cannot recommend it for any business person who is serious about using social media as part of their marketing mix.

Let me explain why by comparing GFC, Ning and a Wordpress blog.

Feature	Google Friend Connect	Ning	Wordpress Blog (self-hosted)
Users sign in	Yes	Yes	Yes
Users have a profile	Yes	Yes	Yes
Allows comments	Yes	Yes	Yes
Allows content rating	Yes	Yes	Yes
Can use polls	Yes	Yes	Yes
Works with e-commerce	No	Yes	Yes
Good for a membership site	No	Yes	Yes
Fully Customizable	No	Mostly	Completely
Useful for list building	No	Good	Excellent
You have complete control	No	Mostly	Yes

This comparison reflects development of each platform as of 15 Oct 09.

Google Friend Connect is a quick and easy way to add a social media dimension to your site. As a business owner, you know that many quick and easy solutions are neither lasting nor effective.

Ning offers a powerful, easy to understand service that is free and outperforms GFC. For anyone using a Wordpress blog, you already have a tool that is unmatched by any other site or service available. There are so many plugins and themes available for Wordpress – and Wordpress continues to work at improving their service – that no one is likely to move them out of the #1 spot.

In all fairness to GFC, it is a new service and Google is still developing it. There was a time when I would have given Wordpress a negative review, too.

Look at the other services Google offers and how well they work. For example, I have two Gmail accounts and like them very much. Google maps is a great tool that I use regularly, and I even like Google Books.

Right now, GFC is a cool toy. When you see the next edition of this guide, you should expect to see a lot more functionality in GFC. When that happens, you can bet I'll show you where it can fit into your social media marketing plan.

Gwave

This service shows a lot more promise than GFC.

GWave is designed to enable you and me to work on projects together. It's a simple concept that a lot of companies are already using so people in different offices across the country, or around the globe, can collaborate on projects.

The big difference between GWave and what the companies are doing is that GWave will be free. The companies have either developed their own platform, or purchased a solution.

GWave allows you to use maps, documents, video, photos, spreadsheets – just about anything you want to build your project.

Let's say the Etobicoke Rotary Club decides to use GWave to plan next year's Ribfest. They have Ribbers, musicians, vendors and a carnival to plan and organize. They also have about 1,100 volunteers to organize, and every member of the Rotary Club is also a business owner.

Imagine being a member of the organizing committee and being able to sit down for 5 minutes in the morning and type in some new information. You don't have to send an e-mail because GWave shows the new information to everyone, and lets them know it was you who added it.

When someone has a map ready for where the Ribbers can place their trailers and the vendors can place their tents, it can be added to the wave easily. Then everyone gets to look it over, make comments or suggest changes, and GWave keeps track of everything. If you ever need to back up a couple of steps, GWave has a record of every change made.

You can even open your wave to the Ribbers and Vendors to let them make comments. GWave keeps track of who makes which changes or comments, so you never have to worry about someone saying "Hey, I didn't say that."

Head over to http://wave.google.com and look at the information they have available. There's even an 80 minute video you can watch.

When you get to the landing page, there is a line near the bottom that lets you request an invitation to GWave. Go ahead and fill in the form for a personal invitation. I filled it in a while ago and haven't received an invitation, but being on the list means I'll be one step ahead of anyone who isn't on the list.

5. Your Social Media Marketing Plan

There's no question Social Media has catapulted into the spotlight and become a serious tool for your marketing efforts.

According to *B2B Magazine* (Association of National Advertisers), the number of advertisers using social media has more than tripled in the last two years, and the number using viral video has doubled. The question is no longer whether you should use social media.

The important question is: Do you know how to use social media to generate profit?

Social Media sites are free to use, but you have to invest your time or an employee's time to make it work. So if it isn't returning a profit for your business, you're just throwing away resources.

That's why we're including this chapter. The best way to use Social Media is to turn it into a 3-way street of communication, and we all need a plan for that.

Most of us are familiar with 2-way communication. I speak to you, you speak to me, and we have a conversation. 3-way communication isn't new – it has just been extremely rare. Social Media has made it attainable for everyone.

What is 3-way communication? You might know it better as Customer Evangelism.

3-way communication is when

1. You speak to your customers
2. Your customers speak to you
3. Your customers speak to everyone else for you

That third element is what we used to call word of mouth advertising.

Word of mouth has been, and always will be, the most powerful form of advertising any business can achieve.

It has also been the most difficult form of advertising to obtain – until Social Media came along.

Now a business can go from obscurity to stardom – or notoriety – in a matter of days. Take Dave Carroll for example.

Dave Carroll is a musician who had a bad experience with United Airlines. He was changing planes at O'Hare Airport in Chicago when he discovered United Airlines baggage handlers literally throwing his band's musical instruments. They ended up damaging Dave's $3,500 Taylor guitar.

After a year of asking United Airlines to make good on their negligence, Dave got tired of asking. He turned to his music and social media to get some satisfaction.

Dave has since recorded two songs about his experience with United Airlines and is in the process of writing and recording a third. The first song has had 5,491,952 views, 35,448 ratings and 22,118 comments (as of 15 Sep 09). His second song is approaching half a million views after being on YouTube for less than a month.

Social Media took Dave Carroll to stardom and has raised the notoriety of United Airlines.

Of course, Dave Carroll already had a loyal following of listeners to share his story with – just like you have a customer base. The entire episode of his guitar being damaged occurred while his band was on tour. Without that following, Dave would have been just another flyer with an airline complaint.

That's what this chapter is all about. We're going to walk through the 3 stages of marketing

1. Outbound Marketing – You Speak to Your Audience
2. Inbound Marketing – Your Audience Speaks to You
3. Customer Evangelism – Your Audience Speaks to Your Audience

and how to use social media to build each one.

It's easy to do. Social media is free so all you need to invest is your time. Let's make the most of your investment and get started on building your business.

You Speak to Your Audience (Outbound Marketing)

There are two primary ways for you to speak to your audience with social media.

1. Blogging
2. Status Updates

As we go along, you'll see there is overlap between you speaking to your audience, your audience speaking to you, and your audience speaking to your audience. Social media isn't structured like a debate or town hall meeting. People are talking everywhere – your objective is to be one of the topics of conversation.

Blogging

Blogging is an excellent example of how the conversations mix. Visit www.michelfortin.com or www.problogger.net (Darren Rowse) and you'll see Michel and Darren speaking out to their audience, people leaving comments to reply, and other people replying to those comments.

Achieving that kind of interaction is your objective.

As successful as Michel and Darren are, they will be the first to tell you that they didn't start out with what they have now.

I don't mean they didn't start out with lots of conversations going on and people interacting with them through social media. They didn't, of course, but they also didn't start out with the blogs they have now. Let me explain…

A blog is nothing more complicated than an online version of a diary or journal. The name "blog" is actually a short form for "web log" or an online diary of events. Webmasters used to use web logs for tracking statistics for web sites, then someone decided it would make a neat way to communicate. It all just developed from there.

Blogging, of course, is you writing something on your blog. What everyone calls "posting."

If you've glanced through the Social Bookmarking chapter, then you know there are dozens of sites that provide you with a blog. You can pick any of them, set up your own blog, and start posting – that's what we're going to talk about here.

Before we do, there is one specific point I'd like to make for everyone who wants to use a blog for their business.

Michel Fortin's blog is also a business website. He sells products from there, has sponsors that pay for advertising space, and links to his other business sites. Michel's blog also comes from Wordpress.

Here's what makes that special: When you go to a site and sign up to use their blogging service, your blog belongs to that site – not you. With Wordpress, you can have a blog that belongs to you.

To do that, you use a free download from www.wordpress.org and your own site hosting account from www.usebluehost.com (or any other hosting company).

The process goes like this:
- ✓ Get a hosting account from www.usebluehost.com
- ✓ Register a domain name for your blog
- ✓ Install the Wordpress blog
- ✓ Start blogging

You know that's a little simplified, but not by much. Wordpress makes installing their software incredibly easy. When I set up my first blog, it took just 45 minutes. (You can always ask your webmaster to do it for you. If you're stuck, I set up blogs for clients. Just send me an e-mail and we'll set it up.)

What's so special about owning your blog? Well, when a blogging site owns your blog they control it. If someone complains about you, your blog can be shut down. When you own the blog, you handle the complaints, and no one can shut you down.

As a business owner, you can see how important it is to have control of your web presence. (Another handy thing is that Wordpress blogs are designed to work well with e-commerce.)

Now let's get back to how you use a blog to speak to your audience.

Whether you make a post daily, once a week, or every Tuesday and Friday doesn't matter as much as being consistent about it.

When you start out, plan to write a blog post just once each week. That gives you plenty of time to think about what you want to write, and put together a good post. Because you're using this for your business, you can't just write about what you did for the weekend.

Writing about what you did for the weekend is fine – it can give you an interesting story – but you have to make it relevant to your business.

Maybe you spent time with your kids and they taught you a valuable lesson about fair play, planning, or how to enjoy getting dirty. Whatever it is, the lesson has to be worthwhile to your audience for you to use it as a blog post. And I don't just mean it's "a good lesson everyone should know." That's the kind of post you make after you have built a loyal following and they're willing to hear your opinions in addition to your expertise.

Making a post relevant to your audience means, in large part, giving them information they can put to use in their lives today. So if you're an accountant, give them information about taxes, debt management or something else related to accounting. Give them what they expect to see from you.

In addition to being regular in your posts and making them relevant, take some time to give them information from someone other than you. How interesting would this guide be if all I did was talk about me?

Find other professionals whose opinions you respect and ask to use their content on your blog. It keeps you from always having to come up with new ideas, and your readers will appreciate that you are giving them more than one viewpoint.

Think of it as getting a second opinion. We all do it, and it doesn't mean we don't respect the first professional. It's just nice to know that someone else (who has the same kind of specialized knowledge) is saying the same thing as the first guy.

That said, you don't always have to use material from people that agree with you. Having spent several years as a carpenter, I know there can be more than one "right" way to get a thing done. So if that's true for what you do, then make a point of sharing information from other professionals who use a different approach than you do.

Your readers will adore you for doing it.

The last thing I'd like to point out is about giving your readers the resources they need.

When you read through any of the books I've written, you'll see that I refer readers to a lot of resources. Some of them have a price and some are free, and they're all something the reader will have a use for.

The idea is that while you're showing your readers how to do a thing, you also give them a link to a resource that helps them do it. It might be something free such as QuickBooks Online, or it might be an information product you have developed and are selling.

My only caution to you is that you avoid having every resource you recommend be something you're selling. When every resource you recommend is one of your own information products, your readers start to wonder if you're writing to help them – or just writing to sell them.

Now let's take a look at your status updates and how to use them.

Status Updates

You can call it a tweet, a ping, a nudge, or just a note.

Updating your status has an incredible power to draw people's attention. Let me share my own story about that.

At the same time that I started writing *friends, followers and Customer Evangelists*, I started tweeting about it. Short, 140 character snippets about what I was doing and why.

Those snippets led to people taking notice and asking questions. Conversations started happening and more people took notice.

My status updates drew attention from some of the Voices of Influence participants and several other people who have helped to promote *friends, followers and Customer Evangelists*. Not bad for a few seconds of typing two or three times a day.

Think of your status updates as a miniature blog post. (Services like Twitter are commonly referred to as micro-blogging sites.)

That means the same guidelines that apply to blogging are good for your status updates. There are a few differences though...

You don't have to be as regular with status updates as you do with blog posts. I aim to send updates in the morning before I start writing, sometime around lunch and again before supper. But it doesn't matter much if I miss one – or even a whole day – or toss in an extra update for something special.

You might also want to combine writing your status updates with commenting on other people's updates. That could make you end up posting several updates if you find a lot of interesting posts from other people.

Staying relevant is important for status updates, too. The difference is what you're staying relevant to.

Status updates are as much, or more, about you as they are about business. These are your opportunity to let your audience see into your life.

When you're writing ad copy, there's a technique called "the Achilles Heel." It means showing a weakness your audience can identify with. It helps them relax and feel closer to you.

Your status updates can do the same thing. Go ahead and write an update about something going wrong. Just keep it light-hearted, turn it into a question, or share the solution.

Of course, it's always better to write about progress you're making, resources you've found and things you've accomplished. Writing about a glitch or problem is a once in a while thing.

Another way to show an "Achilles Heel" is to write about personal events.

Let people into your world by sharing stories about birthdays, children, friends or spouses. Obviously you want to be careful about "sharing too much." The idea is to share the humor and the warmth of the event. Let readers see you have a life beyond your business.

To make posting your status updates easier, use a social media aggregator service such as www.Ping.fm. This type of service allows you to store the login information for all your social media accounts in one place.

Ping.fm has the best selection of services, and is easy to use. They also have some cool add-ons like a toolbar, seesmic video and a mobile application.

Once you login, just type your update, click on the "Ping It" button, and Ping can send out your status update to more than 40 social media sites. This is what lets me update several social media sites in just a few seconds every day.

The next stage of your social media development is having your audience talk with you. Let's take a look at how you can develop your blog and social media profiles into conversational tools.

Your Audience Speaks to You (Inbound Marketing)

I mentioned earlier that there's a lot of overlap with the three stages of marketing. This is where it starts.

Your primary tools for speaking to your audience are also their primary means for speaking back to you.

Your blog and social media profiles are like any business project. You start by speaking to your audience and then build improvements into your blog and expand your social media profiles.

This is what I meant earlier when I said Michel Fortin and Darren Rowse didn't start with the blogs they have today. And no one starts out with anything more than a complete social media profile.

Joining groups, improving your blog and getting people to start speaking to you all take time. There's no way around that.

What we can do is cut down the time it's going to take you to find what you need to improve your blog and show you how to expand your social media presence quickly. As a bonus, we'll also touch on two extra tools you can use to get people talking to you.

Since improving your blog will take the most time and activity, we'll start there.

Improve Your Blog with Plugins

Do you have a favorite blog? If you do, take a second to visit it and do a search for "plugins." A lot of bloggers write posts about the plugins they use.

A plugin is a piece of software that performs a specific function for your blog. For example, Akismet is a popular plugin that blocks spam comments to your blog.

Yes, you can get spam on your blog. So Akismet is a plugin you'll want to use. (Don't worry. It's automatically included with Wordpress blogs.)

The official repository for Wordpress plugins is at www.wordpress. org/extend/plugins. After we talk about two places where you can read about plugins currently in use, you can browse through what's available from Wordpress. I'll warn you, though, that Wordpress has a HUGE list of plugins.

That's why we're going to look at the plugins Michel Fortin uses and the plugins Darren Rowse has recommended. Let's start with Darren.

Darren asked his fellow bloggers to tell him which plugins are their favorites. You can read the list at www.problogger.net/ archives/2005/12/02/word-press-plugins-for-probloggers/.

Something to keep in mind is that these plugins have not been categorized or compared. That means some of the Plugins may do the same thing, or they may not all work together.

Another thing to know is that you don't have to be a programmer to use plugins or modify your blog. Will hiring a specialist make your life easier? Yes, absolutely. But it isn't necessary. I am doing all the work on my own blog and it's turning out the way I want it to be.

That said, I'm also approaching the point where I have planned to stop doing the work myself and hire a specialist. I've done a lot myself because it gives me the understanding and experience I require. And you know that if I can do it – and not seriously break or bungle anything – then pretty much anybody is going to be able to handle making plugins work.

Here's how you use Darren's list: Look for each of the plugins in the Wordpress plugin repository. This will give you the most up-to-date version, and all the plugins listed by Wordpress will work together.

Michel Fortin's post, on the other hand, is an alphabetical listing of every plugin on his blog (active and inactive) complete with a description of what the plugin does. Michel's post is at www.michelfortin.com/wordpress-plugins-michel-fortin-blog/.

Rather than just let you go and explore those two posts and the Wordpress list of plugins, the best way to show you how improving your blog encourages your audience to speak to you is by discussing a couple of those plugins.

The first one to look at is "Add Sig 1.3." This plugin adds a custom signature to the bottom of posts with your author information. You can include a photo, too.

Putting some information about yourself at the bottom of every post might seem a little self-centered. The reason it's good marketing – and a conversation builder – is that it's a consistent reminder of who you are. Remember, the only other thing they have to read in a blog post is the post. There's nothing there about you.

Putting a photo and some information about you helps to keep each post personal. It reminds readers that you're a real person with a face. And keep in mind that it doesn't just have to be about you. Any guest authors on your blog can make use of the plugin to include their own information.

Keep people who make comments on your blog in the loop with "Comment Approved Notifier 1.1."

This plugin sends an e-mail to commentators when you approve their comments. It's always a good idea to hold comments in moderation so you can catch anything Akismet misses. Keeping them in moderation also makes sure you have the opportunity to reply to comments.

Imagine making a comment on a blog and getting an e-mail the next day telling you your comment has been approved. You know that's going to make you feel good because you're getting attention from the blog owner, and you're going to want to go back and look at your comment "in print."

A great plugin for encouraging participation is "Do Follow3.1." Wordpress automatically assigns a "nofollow" attribute to comments. This means search engines don't pay attention to the comments people make.

"Do Follow" removes the "nofollow" attribute so search engines will index comments on your blog. Since every comment contains a link to the commentators own site (if they have one), this means their site gets a better ranking by commenting on your blog. Obviously that encourages people to keep commenting.

You might be wondering how they'll know you have that plugin in place. Simple. Everyone who has a site keep tracks of the statistics for that site. They'll see their comments being indexed by the search engines and recognize the benefit – even if they don't know exactly which plugin you're using to do it.

And the last one we'll look at is "Share This 2.3." This is a powerful plugin that let's your readers share a post or page with their friends. It is very similar to OnlyWire.

Whether you use Share This or OnlyWire, the idea is to make it easy for people to let others know about the great information you're putting on your blog. These services support e-mail, and multiple bookmarking sites.

Okay, one more just because it's a really good one. "Subscribe to Comments" enables anyone who makes a comment to be notified when someone else makes a comment on the same post. This is a plugin that does a lot to promote conversations among your readers.

Now let's have a look at how to expand your social media presence through your profiles.

Expand Your Social Media Presence

You have a profile, and you're posting status updates. The outbound marketing portion of your social media is going well. Now we're going to expand your outbound marketing efforts so they result in some inbound marketing.

The best place to start is with groups. Facebook and LinkedIn offer this feature (as do many other sites) and it's very easy to use. It's a little hard to find on Facebook, but easy to use.

Just so you know, Twitter doesn't have a group feature. There are third party tools you can use to make and manage groups, but Twitter doesn't offer the feature. I'll come back to this at the end of the chapter.

For Facebook, go to your profile and click on the "Info" tab. Scroll down the page until you find your contact information – "Groups" is the next section of the page.

What's that? You're looking but you can't find it? Well, that's a Facebook quirk. It seems that Facebook doesn't tell you about groups, or give you any way to join a group, until after you learn about groups and join some. But it really only seems that way.

In the top right corner of the browser window Facebook has a search window. Type "groups" in there and hit <Enter> or click the magnifying glass. This takes you to a "home page" for groups.

The first thing you see – at the top left of the page – is another search window with the word "groups" in it. You're working your way through a sort of Facebook index. The first search went through the whole site and gave you the Groups page. Now you're going to search through all the groups on Facebook to find some that are of interest to you.

Just click in the box where you see "groups" and type a word or phrase that describes your business or an interest you have.

Pay close attention to the results Facebook gives. The very first thing it lists is not Groups, they list Pages first. A Page is Facebook's way of letting you promote your commercial interests. (We'll come back to this after we look at Groups on Facebook and LinkedIn.)

You can tell a Page quickly because it says "Become a fan" rather than "Join this Group."

Scroll a little farther down the page and you'll see a list of Groups related to your search words. Keep in mind that Facebook has over 250 million users – there are a lot of groups. I typed in "photography" and there are 63,000 groups that relate to photography.

Narrowing it down by typing "digital photography" lowered the number of groups to 4,100. Adding the word "nature" dropped the results even further to 145. So think about what it is you want to search for and use 3 or 4 words to describe it in the search box. You can always broaden your search, and you're better served by finding well targeted groups to participate in.

Start by joining just 4 groups (or fewer). Joining 4 groups on Facebook and another 4 on LinkedIn is going to give you plenty to do in addition to blogging and posting status updates. Remember that this is a business venture – you're going to build up one step at a time and do a good job of it.

Groups on LinkedIn are very easy to find. It's the second item in the menu.

Just click on "Groups" and it takes you to a page that lists the groups you're a member of, any conversations you're following, the Groups directory and a tab where you can create your own group.

Any site that has groups also lets you create your own group. My recommendation is that you spend some time as a group member, watch how others promote and manage their groups, then look at whether you want to create your own.

Think of the groups as though they're a social club in your hometown. If you found a bridge club, bowling league or baseball team that you really enjoyed being a part of, would you go and create your own version or would you get more involved with the group you're already a part of? You're much better served by becoming a leader in an established group than you are by being a leader in an empty room.

Aside from being easier to find, LinkedIn also has a better search function for finding the groups you want to join. Because this is a business networking site, LinkedIn has groups divided into categories such as Corporate, Alumni, and Professional. They have 7 categories including Other.

You can even choose a group based on the language they speak from inside each of the categories.

Again, join a maximum of 4 groups. And let me give you some advice about how to pick the groups.

You have 4 groups on Facebook and 4 on LinkedIn. Start by choosing a group that gives you professional development, and try to find the same group on both sites. For example, I am a member of AWAI's (American Writers and Artists Inc.) groups on Facebook and LinkedIn and a Fan for their Facebook Page.

For now, just choose one group that gives you professional development. You're already doing other things in your business that help you develop, so don't load up on it here.

For your next step, choose one group from LinkedIn and a different group from Facebook that represent your target market. In my case, I have joined two groups for accountants on Facebook and one on LinkedIn. The LinkedIn group is in the professional category, and the groups from Facebook lean toward working with small and medium size businesses.

Joining a professional group gives you a view toward what is on the mind of your target market. More importantly, the professional group gives you a way to contact the people who arrange for speakers at conferences.

The groups you join on Facebook are still oriented toward business, and will have a more relaxed environment than the LinkedIn groups. The groups I have joined are also smaller – only a few hundred members compared to several thousand on LinkedIn. I looked for this because I want to actually make connections with people in the Facebook groups. This is where I have focused my relationship building efforts.

Where you focus your efforts is purely personal choice. I chose Facebook simply because I'm a little more comfortable there. The smaller group size means there is less message traffic so it's easier for me to track what is being said.

So far, you've joined 3 groups. One that's common to LinkedIn and Facebook, and one from each site that is different. Now look for a group on each site that relates to an interest you have.

Yes, you're combining work with pleasure. The fact is, they should never have been separated in the first place. The whole idea that you have to separate work from pleasure came from people who ran crappy workplaces – places where having fun and being healthy just weren't part of the program.

You're about to discover that the most rewarding thing about work is that you can have a lot of fun doing it.

Join a group from Facebook and one from LinkedIn that relate to something you do recreationally. Build relationships in that group and just like any other group you belong to you'll discover connections that promote your business. Then you get to benefit twice – you get business growth and new friendships. (If you don't find one on LinkedIn, you should skip it. Avoid joining an "extra" group on Facebook. That will only increase your workload and distraction level.)

That's probably enough joining for right now. Some readers are going to pause here and some will join a couple more groups. This is something you need to decide on your own based on the time you have available and how comfortable you are with using the sites. Just be careful to keep from overloading yourself.

So now that you're in these groups, what do you do? Is that all it takes to expand your social media presence?

You already know the answer is that you need to participate.

Get involved in conversations, comment on posts, answer questions and ask a few. It's always acceptable to mention what you do as a means for explaining why you're answering. And you don't have to worry about telling people where to find you or your website.

You completed your profile, right? So your website is there for them to see, and they can always send you a message through the site. I can't stress enough that you need to be careful about anything that says "come buy from me."

When you have written a report or article that answers someone's question, it's completely acceptable to tell them about what you've written. Just be sure to give them a useful answer to their question, and suggest they can access the article or report for more detail. The same is true for a book, e-book or audio program.

It's okay to tell people about resources you have produced when you approach it from the point of view that the resource is for more detail. Where you'll draw negative attention is by telling someone you've answered their question but they have to pay for something to get the answer. (It doesn't even look nice when you read it, does it?)

As you participate, give good answers, and show interest in the community, people will be drawn toward you. They'll become inbound to your website, your blog, your profiles and start asking questions.

You'll have outbound and inbound marketing working for you in no time.

The skills you need to reach the point of turning social media into a 3-way street are developing as you get more involved, participate in groups and see what other networkers are doing. You'll see very quickly that it isn't rocket science, and you don't have to be the "Tony Robbins of communication" to make social media profitable for your business.

Before we move on to Customer Evangelism, please let me show you something about
1. Contact pages, and
2. Surveys

A contact page is that page on your website where you put all your contact information. Easy, right? But why just make the page static.

You've seen lots of contact pages on websites where you can send an e-mail to the site owner, or fill in a form to get more information. I have an incredibly simple form on www.theconradhall.com and people send me messages all the time.

You can talk to your webmaster about putting a contact form onto you Contact Page. If you're using www.usebluehost.com for your site hosting, they have several ways for you to put forms onto your webpages, and XSitePro is software I use for creating websites that also gives you form capability.

But what about a way to generate feedback from people who are on your site today?

Good question.

Here's a simple addition you can make to your website to start the ball rolling: On your Contact Page, add a paragraph under your e-mail address that shows visitors why you want to hear from them.

Let them know you're interested in hearing what they have to say, and offer them an incentive to e-mail you. Have a coupon, report or some premium you can send to every person who gives you feedback.

This will do for now to get the ball rolling. You still want to make the effort to put a form onto your Contact Page that lets visitors get in touch with you. And if your website is selling something, then the form should be a lead generation tool as well as a feedback device.

You could even put a survey onto your Contact Page if it's appropriate for your audience. Surveys, however, have a lot more flexibility than just being used on your website.

Before I get too far, let me say www.surveymonkey.com is probably the best supplier of survey services online.

You can develop a survey, put it on a landing page, then drive traffic to it with e-mail, PPC (pay-per-click) and status updates.

Surveys can be used in an Ask Campaign. This is when you plan a teleseminar or other event, and you ask prospects what their most important question is. Alex Mandossian uses these a lot and they are very effective.

More people tend to participate when they get to ask a question, too.

You can even have a survey on LinkedIn or Facebook. Yes. You can put a survey together inside the site and let all your friends and contacts know about it.

In LinkedIn, just click on Applications in the left menu. The Polls application is currently the second one down on the right. They even have a free option, and a paid option for wider distribution.

Facebook has (when I'm writing this) 17 applications that enable you to send polls to your connections.

Since you're on these social media sites to promote your business, use the poll applications to ask people what their biggest need is. Then make the solution and provide it to them.

For smaller problems, you can even give the solution away. Let's say it takes you an hour to type a report that answers one question a lot of people have. Take that report and publish it as an article on www.ezinearticles.com, then post a status update telling everyone about the article.

When you publish one or two articles like that each week, people are going to start paying attention to you and your content.

From content creation to customer satisfaction, surveys are a powerful tool you can easily make use of online – for free. Even www.surveymonkey.com has a free plan that lets you have up to 10 questions on a survey, and they have templates to make creating them easier.

Start with the applications on Facebook and LinkedIn. Using Survey Monkey means you have to have a list to send the survey to, or use a PPC campaign to drive traffic to it. The social media polls get distributed to your contacts, and they'll tell their friends about it – you'll have your first viral content!

Now we're ready to move on to the Customer Evangelism section.

Your Audience Speaks to Your Audience (Customer Evangelism)

There's no question social media has brought a lot of changes to marketing, and it's sure to bring a lot more changes.

One of those changes is the re-naming of the oldest, most-powerful form of advertising ever developed – Word of Mouth. That's all Customer Evangelism is – your customers telling other people good things about you and your business.

One of the many great things about social media is that you can get word of mouth advertising working in your favor faster than ever before.

You've heard of videos "going viral" on YouTube, and marketers who use "viral content" to get people talking about them. The whole idea of something being viral is that word of it gets passed around faster than a bad case of the flu – a virus.

And, like a virus, it's something that spreads so far and so fast, there's just no stopping it.

Everyone's question is: How do you make something go viral?

The answer is simple: make the content relevant and interesting and present it in an attention grabbing way.

Look at Dave Carroll and the attention he has gained from singing about United Airlines. Barack Obama is getting all kinds of attention for calling Kanye West a jackass, and of course Kanye himself is getting a lot of word of mouth advertising.

Rich Schefren also makes use of viral content each time he releases a new free report at www.strategicprofits.com.

Content being viral isn't so much about having a lot of flash or glamour. It also doesn't mean every person in the world – or even most people – will pay attention to it. Being viral simply means the most common method for someone finding out about the content is one person telling another – word of mouth.

Your biggest question is: How do I get people talking about my content?

You already know the biggest part of the answer is to produce relevant content.

You're also getting good at producing relevant content because you've been doing everything from the first two sections of this chapter.

Wait. Let's back up a second. I understand you're probably reading this chapter straight through and making notes. That's cool. As long as you understand that you can't put EVERYTHING in this chapter into action all at once.

Just like Michel and Darren built their blogs up into the masterpieces you see today, you build up your social media presence over time. You might do it in 4 months, or you might do it in a year, but you build up to Customer Evangelism.

Social Media speeds the whole process up, but only CNN makes the news instantaneous.

Read through this section, make notes and plan for how to get customer evangelists, But please don't think there's a magic pill that let's you jump over the beginning stages to get there.

Okay. Back to how you make Customer Evangelism happen.

You know there's more to social media than the Golden Trio – Facebook, LinkedIn and Twitter. These three are good, and I can point you to Jim Turner who uses just these three sites to make his entire marketing plan.

Read that again…Jim doesn't just use the Golden Trio for online marketing – they are his entire marketing effort. And Jim is acquiring new clients steadily.

So you have two options:

A. Keep doing everything from the first two sections and Customer Evangelism will happen. Jim did it in less than a year.

B. Add some other elements to your social media marketing mix to reach a wider audience.

Both are good choices. The determining factor is how much time and energy you have to put into social media marketing.

The more sites you participate in, the more groups you join and the more content you produce, the sooner you're going to reach a point where you need an assistant to help you get everything done. Joining a lot of sites and groups does not automatically translate into business success.

What we're going to do next is look at how to put your social media marketing plan into action. In the process, we're going to look at quite a few sites because I want to cover as much as possible for you. You should feel comfortable picking out what works for you and leaving everything else alone.

You could pick Meetup.com and use only that site – not even bother with the Golden Trio – and still have success. The point is to choose what works for you and focus on that. If you try to participate everywhere, you'll end up like the plate spinning guy who used to be on TV…He would spin a plate on the end of a long stick, and have a couple dozen going at one time.

He couldn't do it for long, and he certainly isn't on TV anymore.

You don't advertise in every newspaper, magazine and phone directory, right? Keep that in mind for social media. You only want to participate in the places where it makes sense for you to participate.

Putting Social Media into Action

The place to start is with the Golden Trio. (That's why it's the Golden Trio and not the silver, bronze or pewter trio.)

The Golden Trio
www.Facebook.com

You have your personal profile. Now you want to put together a Page and, maybe, a Group.

A Facebook Page is where you promote your business on Facebook. Remember, you're not allowed to use your personal profile for commercial purposes.

Creating a Page is simple. Go to any Facebook Page and scroll down the page while watching the left column. At the bottom of the left column is a link that says "Create a Page for My Business." Simply click on that link and follow the steps – it's just like creating a personal profile. The difference is that the information you put in will be all about your business.

A Group on Facebook is slightly different.

A Facebook Page allows you unlimited numbers of fans and you can communicate with them quite freely. Groups are limited to being able to communicate with "just" 5,000 members at a time. That limit isn't a concern for many business owners, but you should be aware of it.

I recommend business owners simply create a Page and drive traffic to it. That avoids ever hitting the limits of a Group.

An excellent resource for getting the most out of Facebook is a blog titled Inside Facebook (www.insidefacebook.com). When you get really serious about using Facebook, they have a report you can buy (naturally). In the meantime, you'll find a wealth of information by looking through their Topics list, Archives, and just by searching the site.

www.LinkedIn.com

Whether you make a Page or a Group on Facebook, go to LinkedIn and make a corresponding Group there.

There are groups I belong to just on Facebook, some just on LinkedIn and a couple that are on both sites. What you're going to do is use the same content for both sites so it really isn't a lot of extra work to have a group on each site. It does bring you a lot of benefit, though.

Think of Facebook and LinkedIn as the two biggest conferences in the world. They run 24 hours a day, 7 days a week, and they reach tens of millions of people every day. Would you like to establish a storefront (group) at just one of those conferences? Or, since it's free, would you like to have a store front at both?

www.Twitter.com

We're going to have to talk about third party applications for this because Twitter doesn't have a group feature.

The first thing to do is read an article from Mashable about creating Twitter groups (http://mashable.com/2009/02/15/twitter-groups-3/). Mashable has a massive collection of resources for social media. If you ever have a question, I recommend starting with a search of their site. Then go to a Google search, and then call someone like me.

A third party application is just like the debit card terminal in a store. You have the store owner (Twitter or another site), the customer (you or me) and the company that provides the debit card terminal (a third party application). In this case, the third party application is adding functionality to Twitter.

I use TweetDeck, and I've looked at TweetWorks. Both are good programs that help you sort through the message traffic on Twitter.

Here's the thing about using Twitter: No matter what you do, there is a lot of message traffic. Jim Turner devotes around 80% of his social media time to conversations on Twitter, and you can easily use Twitter as your primary social media marketing vehicle.

All it really takes is time to sort though the incoming messages, put people you truly want to hear from into groups, and then monitor the traffic stream. Just as in the "real" world, there are lots of people talking in social media. It's up to each of us to sort out who we're going to give our time to and who we're going to tune out.

There is a companion site for Twitter that you should definitely look at if you plan to use Twitter as a major part of your social media marketing. The site is Mr. Tweet (www.mrtweet.com).

Mr. Tweet is incredibly easy to use. It's a third party application that you connect to your Twitter account and then you write recommendations for people you know. You can even ask other people for recommendations, and, of course, they can recommend you without being asked, too.

What's powerful about Mr. Tweet is the authority of the site.

Mr. Tweet's authority comes from recommending people relevant to you, and carefully evaluating each Twitter user. The site discovers people relevant to you by looking at who you're following and who is following you.

When you are following a celebrity, Mr. Tweet will recommend other celebrities. If you follow accountants and authors, then Mr. Tweet is going to recommend accountants and authors. The site is also going to recommend other people who follow accountants and authors.

That's part of their assessment of other Twitter users. I can't claim to know (or even understand) the algorithms they use behind the scenes. What I can claim is that Mr. Tweet is delightfully accurate in pointing me to people I would like to follow. This is a must-have companion site to Twitter.

Your Blog

Personally, I put having a blog ahead of getting started with the Golden Trio. I'm putting it here – after the Golden Trio – because whether you start with a blog, or put it into place later, is entirely personal choice.

Maybe you feel more comfortable starting with the Golden Trio because *friends, followers and Customer Evangelists* gives you step-by-step, illustrated instructions for getting started. That's fine. Someone else might feel more comfortable starting with a blog because their hosting service gives them a one-button setup for Wordpress blogs. That's what www.usebluehost.com does.

The important thing is to have a blog. You can look at Jim Turner's Facebook profile and see that he has 3 blogs.
- ✓ http://jimturnersmm.ning.com
- ✓ http://pitbullmarketing.wordpress.com
- ✓ http://groups.to/nyhvsocialmediafriends

Darren Rowse maintains several blogs on different interests, and although I have only www.TheMarketingSpotlgiht.com, I also write for Technorati and BlogCritics.org.

The social media sites are how people find you. Your blog is where you want them to go. It's the hub for your social media.

Social Media Aggregators

There are more aggregators than the ones I'm mentioning here. Chapter 11 is all about coordinating your social media, and it lists several aggregators. These are just the aggregators I've chosen to use.

That might seem like an odd point to be making. These are the aggregators I use and recommend, but that doesn't mean they're going to be a good fit for you. My recommendation to every client is that they start here, and if these services don't work for them then we look at the others.

www.Ping.fm

I already mentioned Ping once. It's a social media aggregator – Ping collects all your social media into one spot.

Ping uses the same style of interface as Twitter. You have 140 characters to post a status update, and as of 17 Sep 09, Ping supports 37 social media sites. That means you can post a status update to all your social media sites just by typing it into Ping and clicking the "Ping It" button.

This is a great time saver. You do, however, have to be a little bit careful about connecting sites when you use Ping. For example, Twitter and LinkedIn can be connected so all your tweets show up in your LinkedIn profile.

That's great, but if you're using Ping, it will cause duplicate entries to your LinkedIn profile. The "fix" for that little problem is that when you connect Twitter and LinkedIn, choose the option that only posts tweets with the #in hashtag.

I recommend Ping even when a client is only using the Golden Trio. It saves time when you're making general status updates, and doesn't get in the way when you're messaging to individuals.

www.FriendFeed.com

FriendFeed.com is also a social media aggregator, but it has a very different approach.

FriendFeed pulls are your updates, posts and other activity into a single RSS feed. This allows anyone who wants to follow you to stay up to date by subscribing to your FriendFeed.

This is one you should definitely add to your mix because all it takes is the setup time. Once you have connected your other social media accounts to your FriendFeed, everything else is automatic.

www.OnlyWire.com

This one goes with your blog. And while I'm mentioning it, I also want to mention www.ShareThis.com. You'll find both on my blog.

These aggregators let you pull sites into your blog so readers can bookmark your content. This is one way for your audience to talk to other people on you behalf.

OnlyWire has a free and a paid option. (The paid option is only $24.99 per year.) I use the free option, and it means people will see an ad when they use OnlyWire on my site. That's cool by me.

Both services support quite a few sites. You get to choose which ones your readers can bookmark or share your content on. For example, you can choose bookmarking sites such as Tumblr, Digg and Diigo as well as networking sites such as LinkedIn, Facebook and Plaxo.

I recommend putting both of these services onto your blog. All it takes is the effort to put them there, and then they provide you with the benefit of increased reader interaction for forever.

ShareThis even comes as a Wordpress plugin. That makes it super simple to set up.

Niche Sites

These are the other sites listed here in the guide. Sites such as LibraryThing.com and Helpfulvideo.com.

Niche sites are just like Facebook or LinkedIn only, as the name implies, they are focused on a particular interest.

With these sites go all the Ning communities. If you want to find a Ning community related to your business or an interest, simply doing a Google search. For example, an accountant could put "accountants, ning" into Google and come up with several relevant Ning communities.

You definitely want to get involved with relevant niche sites before moving on to use the other types of sites listed here.

Local Networking Sites

This one is left for last because two of the sites have already been covered, and the new site given may well be the best site for local, small business owners to use:

1) LinkedIn
2) Twitter, and
3) Meetup.com

Remember when you completed your profile on LinkedIn that it asked for your zip code (or postal code) on the first page? That's because LinkedIn tries to connect you with people in your community.

If there is a local company you want to connect with, make LinkedIn your first stop. This site is hugely popular among business people so the chances are excellent you'll find someone from that company listed on LinkedIn.

Here is a great article from Mashable that gives 9 ways to find local Twitter users: http://mashable.com/2009/06/08/twitter-local-2/.

My favorite is to do a simple search. I always like simple.

In Twitter, you want to use the name of your town and how far you want to look. For example, you could use "near: Toronto within: 50mi" to find Twitter users within 50 miles of Toronto. It works for any town or city.

Another good one is TwitterLocal (www.twitterlocal.net). This is an application similar to TweetDeck only TwitterLocal tracks tweets from your area. It's easy to use and will help you get in touch with people in specific geographic locations. (You don't have to use it only with your own town if you travel a fair bit.)

www.Meetup.com

For some business owners, there might not be any other site needed to add social media to their marketing mix. Meetup.com might do everything they need.

Meetup is specifically designed to help you organize in-person meetings with groups of people. There isn't a profile to create, and you don't interact a whole lot through the site. Just about all you do is indicate whether you're going to attend an event.

Wayne Cook, from Toronto, has been using Meetup for 5 years with great success. He currently has two groups that meet regularly, several assistant organizers (all volunteers) and several thousand people between both groups. The contacts he has made have allowed him to be in a position to be the first in line to discuss social media with candidates in Toronto's municipal elections. (That's more than 300 candidates and potential clients every time municipal elections happen.)

For a local business owner, your social media marketing plan cannot be complete without this site. Somebody like me or Jim Turner – anyone with a business that can be done over long distances – can use social media without using this site. But for someone who owns a hardware store, barber shop, laundromat or is a tradesperson – you definitely want to use this site.

You can arrange events, publicize them using the internet and traditional media, and build your e-mail list. Meetup is the perfect bridge between traditional marketing and social media marketing.

Bookmarking Serivces

www.Diigo.com

This is my favorite bookmarksite.

When it comes to bookmarking, all these sites are essentially the same. The only reason to use more than one is that they each have their own audience. Yes, there is overlap, but making sure your content is bookmarked on more than one site means you're reaching the widest audience possible.

What makes Diigo my favorite is that it lets me write notes on web pages. It's great. You can highlight text, add comments (they call them annotations), and they stay there after you leave the site.

You can also make your highlighting and comments public, but I don't recommend that. In fact, I tell people I'm coaching to keep all their annotations private and to use the Diigo menu to hide public annotations.

After all, if you have something worthwhile to contribute to a site, don't you think the person who owns the site would appreciate an e-mail more than you putting a "sticky note" on their web page? Sending them an e-mail means you get to make a new contact, and you're showing that person you genuinely care about the quality of their site. (I very much do not like public annotations from Diigo users.)

As you can imagine, I use the note function to mark a web page while I'm researching. Then I can either print that page with the notes, or just keep it bookmarked for easy reference.

www.Digg.com

The way to use this type of site is by bookmarking content you put onto the internet. When you write a good blog post, you bookmark it here so other people can find it. You can do the same thing when you add a new page to your site, or add important information.

At the same time, send a status update to your network to let them know about the new bookmark. As they have a look at the content, they can bookmark it, too, and that increases the ratings for that content. Higher ratings mean more people will see it.

www.Technorati.com

Also a social news site, Technorati is a trend setter – and watcher – for the internet community.

Technorati maintains an objective list of the top 100 blogs on the internet, and is possibly the most frequently accessed social news site today.

As with all the sites I'm listing here, Ping can update your status with Technorati, too. What Ping does with any social news site is post any links you submit in your updates. So a plain text update about finishing a project won't get posted to the social news sites – it doesn't fit what those sites want.

When you post an update with a link in it, the link gets sent to the social news sites.

www.Delicious.com

This is a cool service because it stores your bookmarks with keywords and a description that you write in yourself. It also has a toolbar you can add to your browser so it coordinates the bookmarks in your browser with the bookmarks you send to Delicious.com.

Video Sites

One of the great things about video is that it doesn't take a lot of time.

There's more detail about this in <u>Chapter 9 – What is Video Sharing</u>, and <u>Appendix C – Video Resources</u>. For now, it's enough to say that once you put a video into place on your site, you can pretty much forget about it. It doesn't take a whole lot of maintenance.

www.YouTube.com

You probably already know about YouTube. It's a video sharing site, and the largest one of its kind.

Having an account with YouTube allows you to post any videos (less than 10 minutes long) you produce quickly and easily. In case you're thinking "I could never produce a video," let me show you how easy it is.

I have a Sony Cybershot pocket camera. It shoots video as well as takes still photos. I have used my cybershot to record and post more than two dozen videos – and each one took longer to record than it took to post it to the internet.

Believe me, shooting video is far easier than you imagine. When you think you're ready to give it a try, drop me a line and we'll chat (<u>Conrad@theconradhall.com</u>).

You definitely want to have a YouTube account. Even if you don't use it a lot – I don't use mine a whole lot, yet – you want to get your account now. The main reason is that usernames have to be unique. If you wait, then you might not get the name you want.

www.MotionBox.com

This is a great companion site for YouTube because it lets you do all your editing.

I don't have a program on my computer for video editing, so I use MotionBox. The editor is very easy to use, files upload quickly to the site, and there aren't any limits on how much you can upload each month. Of course, you can also keep your videos on the site and display them there, too.

Your username doesn't matter quite so much on this site, but I still recommend getting an account at the same time as you get a YouTube account. You're more likely to end up with the same username, and that's a good thing. Having the same username across all the sites you use makes you easier to find.

www.Viddler.com

This is also a video sharing site, but I'm mentioning it for everyone who plans to use video on the internet.

Viddler is specially designed to give your videos professional polish, and make them friendly toward search engines. It isn't a free service for businesses, but it does provide a high level of value.

Viddler is an excellent tool for any business that is providing online videos to customers. For example, AWAI uses Viddler to host videos they use for online training.

So when you have a short video you want to use for driving traffic or spreading a message, use YouTube. After someone has come to your site and subscribed to something that uses online video, use Viddler to host those longer videos.

Information Sharing Sites

These are similar to your blog, but they can be more static. Where you'll be updating your blog daily or weekly, you can update these sites once a month or even every couple of months.

Setting up a page on one of these sites is similar to creating a group on LinkedIn or a Page on Facebook. The difference between the two is that information sharing sites tend to be viewed more as reference tools than places to network.

The three biggest information sharing sites are:

1. www.Squidoo.com
2. www.Hubpages.com
3. www.wiki.com

The reason I'm not splitting these out and giving a description for each is that they each do the same thing. You go to the site and create a page that's all about your specialized knowledge.

Squidoo calls it a Lense, HubPages calls it a Page and Wiki just calls it an entry (or a Page).

People can certainly interact with you on these sites. Squidoo was developed by Seth Godin as a means for smaller publishers to distribute their content. Obviously, that kind of use wants a site that allows interaction with readers.

The other reason for not going into detail here is that, by the time you're ready to make use of information sharing sites, you won't have much need for someone to explain them to you. You'll be completely familiar with social media, how sites work, and the content you want to use.

6. A Social Media Case Study

Everything is easier when you have an example to follow. Tradesmen learn by apprenticeship, doctors learn by internships, and even an iPod comes with illustrated instructions.

It only makes sense to give you an example to follow in social media. Finding the right example, though, was a little more difficult than you might imagine. After all, with social media being "all the rage" and experts popping up like tulips in spring, you'd think there'd be at least dozens of good examples, right?

I thought so, too.

There are definitely lots of examples of successful people and companies in social media. David Meerman Scott and Seth Godin are best-selling authors on the topic and successful users of social media. They are good role models for me.

That was the key to finding the right example – it had to be a role model almost everyone can use and follow.

The choice couldn't be a person or company who's already a blazing success. Big successes make nice show-pieces and good motivators, but they're too far separated from those of us who are just getting started.

Any example has to be
- ✓ an entrepreneur
- ✓ a business owner
- ✓ someone <u>without</u> massive resources, and
- ✓ someone who started out with an interest but very little knowledge

I looked for someone who is achieving measurable results, but isn't so far ahead of the rest of us that his success seems intimidating.

You can understand how finding the right example was a little tough. And I have to admit that I didn't find the right example – he found me.

My first contact with Andrew Ballenthin was in relation to a book he is writing. He was looking for people with experience and knowledge of social media, and I volunteered to answer questions. That was in September,

2009, and it was in November, 2009 that Andrew sent an e-mail asking me to be a judge for a blogging competition he was hosting.

That certainly caught my interest, so Andrew and I spoke on the telephone. I agreed to be one of the sponsors for Blog Off II with the idea of seeing how it worked and whether it would make a good example. (Being a sponsor also seemed like it would be easier than being a judge.)

You guessed it...I ended up thoroughly impressed with Andrew, the team he put together, and the feedback I'm getting from the competitors.

Let me step back for a second and give you some of the history of Andrew and the Blog Off Competition.

History of the Blog Off Competition

Andrew started blogging in May 2008. (He definitely isn't one these "I invented the internet" types.) He started with the objective of developing his reputation for Thought Leadership in the realm of marketing and social media.

The online industry is new enough to accommodate all comers, and Andrew has a long history in traditional marketing, so moving into social media is a natural progression for Andrew. Aside from self-promotion, he needs to know how to use social media so he can effectively serve his clients.

He hosted the first Blog Off Competition in May 2009 – after being an active blogger for only 12 months – with the goal of developing a *"microcosm of what is happening in the wider online environment."*

By the end of that first venture, Andrew had
- ✓ Recruited 11 part-time writers for his blog
- ✓ Developed a large LinkedIn network
- ✓ Gained access to an audience of more than 1 Million readers
- ✓ Legitimized the social media industry with measurable results, and
- ✓ Built a brand-new social media community with a pay-it-forward attitude

Blog Off II ran from 1 December '09 to the 12th.

For his second effort, Andrew went from 15 competitors to having competitors from 6 countries. He also went from being all alone to having a team of 15 seasoned marketing and social media professionals (including himself). Through his team, Andrew's audience has increased to over 6 Million readers and listeners, and he has drawn the attention of Huffington Post, Agora Media, Six Apart and Your Business Channel, BlogTalkRadio.com, ThatChannel.com, and Canoe.ca.

This is where we start looking at what Andrew has done and how to apply it to your business.

The Starting Point

Andrew started by realising he had a need to learn about social media.

Social media is too large a phenomenon to ignore. It's different from TV or radio because social media doesn't represent a new technology. It's still just using computers and the internet.

Social media is to advertising, marketing and even journalism what the iPod is to music and radio. Social media allows the consumer to decide what he or she will consume.

On television, a commercial comes on and you either pay attention or you don't. In social media, marketers go to great lengths to make sure any ad you see is relevant to the content of the web page you're visiting. Whether you click on an ad tells the advertiser if they're getting it right.

It's the same for stories or news on any site. Let's say I write a blog about creating information products and marketing them (www. TheMarketingSpotlight.com) – which I do. You're a loyal reader and stop by once each week to catch up on what I've written.

One day you make your regular visit and find a series of articles about how much I like Habitat for Humanity, and how good their projects are. They're all good articles, and the content is entirely correct, but is that why you're visiting The Marketing Spotlight? No.

This isn't a newspaper where you expect to find lots of different content in the various sections. The Marketing Spotlight is a blog dedicated to providing accurate, useful information about creating information products and how to market them.

Anything else I want to write about belongs on a different blog, or in a relevant group on one of the social media sites.

In Andrew's case, he wanted to extend his reputation for being a good marketing consultant into the online world. But he didn't just want to be good, he wanted to develop a Thought Leadership position in social media marketing. That means he has just a couple of years to move from being a newcomer, to being someone you and I look to for information and advice on using social media effectively.

So Andrew started learning and building a network.

He chose LinkedIn for his starting point because it is a business networking site. It just made sense to look for contacts, and develop a reputation, on the site that is most densely populated with prospective partners and clients.

Whether LinkedIn is going to be the best spot for you to start building a network depends very much on the kind of person you're looking to connect with. If your business is all about knitting and crafts, then dailymotion.com or Facebook might be better choices for you.

There are two keys for any business person wanting to make the best use of marketing/advertising in general, and social media in particular.

1. Think through who you want to connect with.

There are at least two kinds of people you should be describing:

1. Clients
2. Partners

Andrew was fortunate to be able to find both on the same site. You might look for partners on LinkedIn and clients on other sites.

When I say "think through," I mean write down as much detail about each person as possible. When I work with clients, I have a worksheet they fill out that covers the demographics and psychographics for an ideal prospect (client or partner). It even goes all the way to asking you to give your prospect a name.

The better your mental picture is of who you want to find, the more likely you are to find them. For example, when you're looking for a partner what is it you're looking for?

One of the aspects Andrew has deliberately looked for is being an Industry Influencer. Because Andrew is growing the Blog Off competitions, it isn't enough for him to find people who are good at what they do. He needs to find leaders; people good at what they do who also influence others to follow them.

2. Find someone to help you learn.

"Learn" is practically a four-letter word in marketing. It suggests having to work, and that's generally the last thing you want to tell someone – that they're going to have to work to get results.

Just look at any magazine and see how all the ads say you can do something with little or no effort. Diet ads are the best for this – they'll tell you it's possible to lose weight and "be beautiful" while munching chocolate cake and doing zero exercise. You just need their product.

Maybe what they're saying is true, but social media is a highly personal experience – for you and your prospects. It isn't like trusting a marketing consultant to make a good space ad for you.

Social media is going to spotlight your personality and that of your business…especially when you're a small business owner. After all, for most of us, being a small business owner means we are the business.

We'll come back to this again when we look at how Andrew built his team. For now, keep it in mind that you need to find someone to learn from and work with.

A Test Run

Remember that Andrew started blogging in 2008. He founded the Community Marketing Blog (www.CommunityMarketingBlog.com) and started sharing what he knew.

Just 12 months later, Andrew had organized and launched Blog Off I.

He had 40 entrants which he qualified down to 15 competitors from 4 countries, and was doing the evaluation all by himself. At this point, he understood metrics but was working out how to apply traditional marketing metrics to social media. It wasn't easy, but as I mentioned at the start of this chapter, Andrew got some great results.

Because he got those good results, Andrew invested more time and energy into learning and building his network. He made more contacts and planned a larger event – Blog Off II – based on his initial success.

You can see how social media is just like any other business enterprise. You try something and see how it goes. When you get success, you make a few tweaks, and do it again on a larger scale. If it falls flat, you look for a new approach and try again.

Since Andrew had a resounding success (credit goes to his having made a good plan to start with), he decided to go straight to growing his team. The Blog Off idea didn't really need any tweaking, but Andrew knew – and knows – he needs a team to keep building on the success.

Online Team Building

This is where you'll start seeing some difference between traditional networking and social networking (or online networking).

Your online network is going to be much larger than any network you can build through traditional networking. It's also going to be much more collaborative in nature, and have a greater element of trust and mutual support.

When you meet someone at a conference or trade show, you have that personal interaction to help you judge whether you want to work with someone. Of course, that personal interaction can also be a stumbling block that keeps you from working with someone who could be a great partner or client.

In the world of social media, it doesn't matter if you stutter, have poor fashion sense, eat raw garlic for lunch or are introverted. Because you're functioning from the comfort and security of your own office, you can easily overcome things that are "networking killers" in any traditional setting.

And because it's incredibly easy to "turn someone off" in the online world, everyone has to behave well to maintain their network.

Let's say you meet someone at a conference and trade business cards. After the conference, you get a package in the mail filled with their marketing message. A couple days later, the telephone calls start…two or three times a week, every morning at 9:15 sharp, this person calls to ask how they can make your life easier.

Which we can all translate into "how do I sell you something so I can move on to the next pigeon?"

Because this contact came through traditional networking, the only way to stop the calls is for you to deal directly with the person. You have to tell them you don't appreciate the interruptions.

In social networking, slamming a new acquaintance with marketing materials can get you reported for spamming, disconnected from their network, kicked out of a group, and even banned from a site. That's why most of the people you meet through social networking have a pay-it-forward, collaborative attitude – á la Dale Carnegie's *How to Win Friends and Influence People*.

To give you an idea of what you can do to build you own online team through networking, let's take a look at the team Andrew put together to help him with Blog Off II.

Just before we start, let me clarify that Andrew was looking for people to help him

✓ Promote the competition (sponsors),
✓ Judge the competitors, and
✓ Provide post-event media publicity

The next stage of growth for the Blog Off Competition means Andrew will be looking for team members to help him organize and lead the project.

He has a team for prize sponsors, media sponsors, media contacts and judges. Now he will look for people who can help him continue to grow and improve that team. Again, it's just like any other business enterprise – or any other project. You build one piece, one step, at a time.

Now let's look at Andrew's team. (Because I don't want to make any one person or position seem more important than another, everyone is listed in alphabetical order by their last name.)

Ballenthin, Andrew (Organizer)

It might seem funny to list Andrew as part of his own team, but I'm sure you see the importance. (Although it is rather funny that his last name also puts him first in the list!)

Andrew is leading the team. In your business, you're going to be leading your team – you're the business owner. In the initial stages of growth, your energy and enthusiasm are going to be vital for gaining success.

Even when you hire someone to come in to show you and your staff what to do, it will be your approval – you lending credibility – that goes a long way toward making the consultant effective.

Until Andrew brings in other leaders to "share the load," he has to stay out front and lead the way. That's why he's looking for those other leaders now.

Hall, Conrad (Prize & Media Sponsor)

Being a sponsor usually means giving something of value to the event. In this case, the act of giving has quickly resulted in benefit to the giver.

This chapter – showcasing Andrew and the Blog Off Competition – is what I gave to Andrew. You can definitely see how giving this to Andrew also makes this entire book more effective. After looking across the internet for 4 months, I'm convinced this is the best possible example of a business owner using social media effectively.

Thank you, Andrew, for asking me to be involved. And for letting me write about your growth and success.

Hansen, Jon (Prize Sponsor & Judge)

Jon's focus is supply chain management, logistics, industry trending and social media. He hosts the <u>PI Window on Business</u> talk show on Blog Talk Radio, and is the author of *Your Show Will Go Live in 5 Seconds*.

Jon's involvement instantly increased the audience size for Blog Off II by 1 Million listeners.

Hill, Leon (Prize & Media Sponsor)

Leon is the founder of USocial.net. This is a social media advertising service launched 1 December 2008 and based in Australia.

You can see how having a team member whose specialty is promoting through social media is valuable to a social media based event.

Hoving, Allan (Prize Sponsor)

Allan is a social media consultant with GetSocial New Media Marketing and a co-host with Jim Love and Janet Fouts on Game Changing, a Blog Talk Radio show.

Jenkins, Andrew (Judge)

Andrew specializes in business design and innovation with emerging technologies at Volterra Consulting. He is also a contributing author for the Community Marketing Blog.

Kirkland, Ginevra (Media Contact)

Ginevra is the Community Manager at Six Apart Media. She was also one of the media contacts for the Blog Off Competition.

Her focus is building community (a key element in Andrew's plans) and creating clear, consistent two-way communications between you and your customers. Ginevra has promoted the competition through Six Apart's network on their home site, Twitter and Facebook.

Love, Jim (Prize & Media Sponsor)

Jim is the CEO at Chelsea Consulting and a faculty member at University of Waterloo. He is also a co-host of Game Changing on Blog Talk Radio.

Allan and Jim featured Andrew and the Blog Off Competition on their show and helped increase audience participaton.

Magaro, Tami (Media Contact)

Tami is a social media strategist at Mindeliver Media and one of the media contacts for the Blog Off Competition.

Tami brings years of experience in television broadcasting (as a producer and director) to the team.

McClure, Mike (Prize Sponsor and Judge)

Mike is the Executive Creative Director at The Yaffe Group and specializes in TV and Video creation.

Mike has a gift for connecting with clients and helping them reach their goals using traditional and social media. His communication and networking skills have been tremendously useful in spreading the word about Blog Off II.

Morris, Ted (Judge)

Ted specializes in thinking outside the box and is a contributor to the Community Marketing Blog.

His experience in customer satisfaction measurement and marketing strategy are an important part of developing the measurements for the Blog Off Competition. A big part of the competition is being able to show business owners that social media can be measured, and you can track your social media ROI (return on investment).

Rutledge, Patrice-Anne (Judge)

Patrice is the author of 27 books, a business technology expert, and a communications consultant. She has been interviewed by CNN, Fox News, AOL and other media outlets.

She knows how to craft and deliver a message. That makes Patrice an ideal candidate for judging the Blog Off Competition.

Sharma, Shradha (Prize & Media Sponsor)

Shradha is an international team member from India. She is the founder of Yourstory.in – a site designed to provide a platform for entrepreneurs online.

Shradha's traditional network is as valuable as her online network to helping the Blog Off Competition grow and develop.

Sinclair, Mark (Prize & Media Sponsor & Judge)

Mark is also an international team member. He is from the United Kingdom and is the Features Editor at yourBusinessChannel.com. Mark is also the Managing Director at Hubbub (UK) Limited.

Mark specializes in "always looking for connections." He gave a tremendous boost to Blog Off II by introducing the competition to his more than 5 Million viewers.

Tyios, Julie (Judge)

Julie is the CEO for Red Juice Media and the Marketing and Community Manager at Vestiigo (a new Canadian career site).

In addition to the specialties each team member brings to the table, they were all active in promoting Blog Off II through their social networks. That means they tweeted about it in advance, and during the competition. They also started discussions on LinkedIn and Facebook groups.

Wherever possible, each team member mentioned the competition on their blogs, in their e-zines, and even in e-mails.

Will all of these team members stay with Andrew and continue to build the Blog Off Competition? The answer is: probably not.

Just like any team, it will grow and change. Each of these people is volunteering their time and energy. So while there is no question that they will stay connected to Andrew and be supportive, being directly involved depends more on their schedule and availability than it does on desire.

You should be looking for the same kind of process in your social network. There will be lots of people willing to answer questions for you, but patience is needed. When someone is volunteering their expertise, it may be a few days before they are able to respond.

When you find someone you would like to partner with, be sure you understand how they will benefit, too. Be sure to show them the benefits involved, and do what you can to make it easy for them to participate.

For example, before and during the competition, Andrew and I supplied the team members with pre-written Twitter messages. They also received directions for how to use them.

Each message had a "release window" with it. That is, a space of a few days when the message could be used. Every message also had the #blogoff2 hashtag in it. This allowed everyone to search for the hashtag and retweet each other's messages.

That coordination and cooperation in communicating with our audiences resulted in more than 27,700 page views, 110 blog posts and 1,262 comments for the competition. It also gave us almost double the number of competitors that participated in Blog Off I.

Let me go back to a point I made under *Find Someone to Help You Learn.*

> *Social media is going to spotlight your personality and that of your business…especially when you're a small business owner. After all, for most of us, being a small business owner means we are the business.*

Having people on your team who understand the shape of your business now, and what you want it to look like 5 years from now is useful and important. You want individuals who are going to help you find spots for improving, and strengths you can use for building on.

In every case, what you are looking for is someone who agrees with your basic philosophy and personality. This doesn't mean you're looking for "yes-men." As John Maxwell says *"It's lonely at the top* [being a leader], *so you'd better take someone with you."*

That means you surround yourself with people who have similar attitudes and characters. For example, a high-energy person should look for other high-energy people to work with. Being paired with a low-energy person is going to drive both of you cuckoo.

Does that mean your teammates will occasionally disagree and tell you you're wrong? Yes. That's part of what makes them valuable. For a detailed study of leadership, and how to do it well, I recommend reading John C. Maxwell's *21 Irrefutable Laws of Leadership.*

Now let's take a look at the competitors and how they benefited. We'll also tie it back in to the growth and development of the Blog Off Competition.

Benefiting the Competitors

The most obvious benefit is the opportunity to take home a share of $45,000 in prizes. This includes a branding consultation, citation here in *friends, followers & Customer Evangelists*, being interviewed on the online radio and television shows represented, and being featured on all of our blogs and e-zines.

But that's really just the surface of the benefits to competitors. Let me share some of the comments competitors sent to me:

> *Anytime there is an opportunity to learn it is worthwhile. Writing under pressure provides an opportunity to see how well you can perform under those conditions and measure your competence against others. Yes, I would compete again.*
>
> –Sue Leonard

> *…the experience of participating in the Blog-Off II contest was a good one. I am a freelance animator/ cartoonist, I spend a lot of time alone. Since going digital many years ago, writing has not been a priority. Participating in Blog-Off II is kind of like entering a tournament. It gives you a chance to focus on a skill and socialize with other creatives.*
>
> –Mike Browne

> *This competition was a learning experience for myself and the reason being is because I have never wrote a blog before nor have I been in a competition with so many talented individuals.*
>
> *I read every single blog, and commented on at least 90% of them, some comments were how to improve on a readers aspect and other comments were about the actual content and how I have related to it. I have learned how to create eye catching titles, produce relevant content and how to market the blog in itself. I benefited from the blog in many aspects, one of which being that I was able to*

create new friendships that I would have otherwise not been able to create if this contest was not there.

—3rd Place Blog-Off Winner Tim Ruffner

One of the key learning points for me during the competition was the power of social media and social networking to drive action.

By focussing my efforts on the communities that I built, and that I cultivated for the last two years through sharing value, I was able to move a significant number of people to take action and view my posts. By being engaged in these communities, understanding the content that they would respond to, and the types of headlines that would engage them I had an audience ready to respond and take action when leveraged."

—1st Place Blog-Off Winner Sean Nelson

I know from having chatted with the competitors that each one found the competition a positive experience. They also spotted areas where improvements and modifications can be made.

In my opinion, the single biggest indicator of success for Andrew's Blog Off Competition is that every person involved – judge, sponsor or competitor – feels comfortable making suggestions for improvement. They are part of a community, feel ownership for that community, and recognise that they will be heard – and heeded – by the organiser.

This is what you're after when building a social network around your business.

Let's use my favourite example when it comes to social media: the hardware store owner.

We'll use Jane and Jim. They own a hardware store – say an Ace Hardware store – in a small town. There are 12,000 people in the town, and it's surrounded by farms. What good can it possibly do for Jane and Jim to build a social network and give their customers what they want?

(Don't you just love it when the answer is right there in the question?)

Social media isn't about using some new, fantastic marketing method. For business owners, it's about communicating – having a conversation – with your customers. It's about using the medium your customers want to use.

One day, Ace Hardware adds a paint to their inventory that primes and covers in one coat. Would this be useful to some of Jim and Jane's customers? Probably.

Has Home Depot demonstrated the value of hosting "how-to" seminars for customers? You bet.

Is now a good time for Jane and Jim to develop a Facebook fan page for their business where they can invite customers to just such a "how-to" seminar? Hmmm…Let me think…

Of course it is.

You can see why using social media is often called Relationship Marketing. You're a small business owner, and if you've been in business for any length of time you're already a Relationship Marketing expert.

The only difference between what you've been doing and using social media is getting to know the online environment. Your customers stop and chat with you in your store because they want to.

They'll join your group, become a fan, or give you their e-mail address for the same reason: They want to hear what you have to say.

Your customers trust you to give them useful, accurate information. By using social media, you're simply giving them another way to receive it.

The competitors in Blog Off II benefited because they wanted to learn more about how to use social media. In the process, several of them have developed friendships and even partnerships.

Three of the competitors have told me they are continuing to work together to build their own social media marketing plans and strategies. Several of the competitors have asked me about coaching them in social media, and of course the top performers will be invited to be ongoing contributors to the Community Marketing Blog.

Top Performers in Blog Off II

Before leaving this chapter, let's have a look at the top 3 performers from Blog Off II.

You can find all the participants – judges, sponsors and competitors – in Appendix F. You'll also find the URLs (web addresses) for their social media profiles there.

The profile for each of the top performers from Blog Off II contains stats. Just so you know, the stats I've used are weighted, or cumulative, stats for each person. Andrew Ballenthin did all the math so competitors that posted several times had no more or less advantage than someone who only posted twice.

Here are the top performers from Blog Off II:

1^St *Place*
  Sean Nelson   http://www.sonarconnects.com

2nd *Place*
  Sam Diener   http://www.samdiener.com

3rd *Place*
  Tim Ruffner   http://www.linkedin.com/in/timruffner

Sean Nelson (http://www.linkedin.com/in/seannelson)

Sean is an author, blogger, speaker and trainer at SONARconnects (www.sonarconnects.com). He is also the owner of XL Benefits and Atlanta Health & Life (www.atlantahealthlife.com).

Over the last two years, Sean has successfully blended his experience and professionalism in the insurance industry with social media. One of the results he has achieved is to become the #1 Atlanta Insurance Professional on LinkedIn.

In Sean's own words:

> *"The end result is that now I help small businesses and professionals with their employee benefits or health insurance needs and I help them understand how to use social media to drive new business."*

He's a perfect example of how a small business owner can use social media to increase the customer base *and* develop a new revenue stream.

Sean made two posts during Blog Off II. Both focused on LinkedIn and how you can use it well.

The first post described the seven most common mistakes Sean has seen people make on LinkedIn. He also gave the fixes for those mistakes. You can read the post at http://bit.ly/8X55Jm. (The actual URL is about 3 lines long, so I'll be using bit.ly URLs.)

The second post outlined four LinkedIn strategies, their strengths and even (gently) their weaknesses. Read the post at http://bit.ly/5TiKNh. More importantly, Sean closed the post by discussing what he calls the Process of Familiarity.

For me, this drove home the point that social media is not a "magician's hat" for marketing. Running out and connecting to thousands of people on various social media sites is not going to automatically – or even necessarily – help grow your business. It might actually do your business harm.

Social networking, as I have said before, is no different from traditional networking. Yes, there are more bells and whistles, but someone you connect with online is no more likely to do business with you than someone you meet at a local Rotary Club meeting.

Wherever you do your networking, it takes time to develop a relationship. It is the relationship (remember the term Relationship Marketing!) that will give someone reason to do business with you.

Sean made his understanding for the value of relationships clear during Blog Off II. He showed the value he places on relationships again when Andrew asked Sean to comment on the experience of competing in Blog Off II.

Here is what Sean had to say:

> *One of the key lessons the contest reinforced was the power of social media to convey a message and to generate a response.*
>
> *Writing the Social Media Sonar blog has helped me build my brand on the various social media/ networking sites. When it came to the contest I simply tapped into these networks and benefited from the credibility I've built up over the last two years. I was also able to connect with some of the other contestants, although between promoting the blogs, the short contest duration, and everyday work, I didn't interact as much as I had hoped.*
>
> *In the end the results I achieved were based on tapping into what I call the 4 C's of social media…. Communities, Content, Conversations, and Conversion. I tapped into the various communities, sharing the blog posts, and asking them to add their thoughts. In this case the conversation was the conversion.*

Something to pay attention to for both of Sean's posts is how he responded to comments. He used a mixture of direct response and "comment roundup."

Remember that the comments you generate, and the replies you make, are perhaps the biggest element of social media. They form the conversations that build relationships. And it doesn't really matter if the comments are on a blog post, a Facebook wall or made via Twitter.

Direct response replies work well when someone has made a specific comment that you want to reply to. I've used it myself on several occasions when there was an opportunity to explain a process or reason to answer a question in detail.

One drawback to direct response is that you might need to be in a timely position to respond. This depends very much on where you have your blog hosted.

For example, my Wordpress blog allows me to respond directly to a comment and my reply appears with the comment. So even if it's a week before I write my reply (which I hope never happens – very bad form), that reply will still appear with the original comment.

Other services such as Blogspot and Blogger use an in-line system for comments. If a week has gone by before you reply to someone's comment, then there will be a week's worth of comments between your reply and what you are replying to.

This is where "comment roundup" is very handy.

During Blog Off II, comments came in very quickly and were often short. Questions could generally be answered with one or two sentences, and many of the comments Sean received could be answered with "Thank You" or an expression of agreement.

A comment roundup allows you to start each paragraph with the name of the person to whom you are replying. You then make your response and invite further conversation.

You can even use a comment roundup to begin replying to a particular person, and indicate you'll provide a more detailed answer later. That answer can be in the form of another reply, or you might choose to use your expanded answer as a new blog post.

Here are the weighted stats that show the success of Sean's approach. Readers of the Community Marketing Blog
- ✓ Viewed Seans' posts 5,157 times
- ✓ Spent an average of 4.5 minutes reading, and
- ✓ Made 93 comments.

I'm using the weighted stats Andrew Ballenthin provided to the judges so you can compare apples with apples.

One of the key tactics that gave Sean success in Blog Off II is that he leveraged the relationships he has built through social media. This is incredibly important for every business owner.

When you enter the social media arena, you are not looking for a brand new audience. Yes, you want to expand your audience – everyone wants to grow their business. But start in social media by communicating with people you already know.

That's why all the social media sites consistently urge you to connect with people you know.

Let's say you're a hardware store owner (my favorite example) and you've decided to start using social media. You set up accounts with the Golden Trio (Facebook, LinkedIn and Twitter), and you connect with everyone you have an e-mail address for in Outlook.

Who are the people you have e-mail addresses for? They're family, friends, long-time customers, business associates and other people you know fairly well, right?

Of course, just by getting an account with each of the Golden Trio sites you're going to have new people notice you. That's fine, and take advantage of the attention by connecting with new people.

But your hardware store makes sales by catering to the people who live nearby. You're already communicating with those people through traditional media and networking, so use that existing network to spread the word about your new social media efforts.

Just as Sean told his contacts that he was competing in Blog Off II and wanted their support, you can tell your contacts that you're getting started with social media. Offer them a choice of premiums when they introduce another local to you on one of the social media sites.

For example, Sam connects with you on Facebook and says that Joe told him about your new communication strategy. That means you give Joe a choice of premiums – golf balls, BBQ tools or garden seeds. Naturally the premiums you choose are based on knowing what your friends enjoy.

You can make it a Tweetup (a gathering organized on Twitter), and combine it with a food drive or other charitable effort. When people arrive, give them a coupon when they quote a keyword you only gave out using social media. And make a point of taking photographs during an event so you can post them to Facebook to share the fun.

One last thing I'd like to mention about Sean before moving on is a tool he has developed for measuring the effectiveness of your LinkedIn profile and participation. He calls it the Linkulator.

You can find the tool at http://bit.ly/6G2zoz.

It takes about 30 seconds to fill in the questions and get a score. When I used the Linkulator, my LinkedIn profile and level of participation earned me a score of 59.5.

While that puts me above the average credibility score, it also shows I have lots of room to improve my performance on LinkedIn.

Go ahead and check your own score. Send me an e-mail to let me know how you're doing, and we'll see if we can work together to make both our performances better.

Sam Diener (http://www.linkedin.com/in/samdiener)

Sam is the founder and creative strategist for Stuff For Success – the blog Sam hosts at www.samdiener.com.

Sam is also the newest social media participant who competed in Blog Off II. At the time of the competition, Sam had been active in social media for only 4 months.

During those 4 months, Sam was able to garner 40,000 page views from 91 countries, made guest posts on the Personal Branding Blog and Under30CEO, and became one of the rising social media stars in the Philadelphia area.

What I find most interesting about Sam's entry into social media is that he had the foresight to partner with an editor when he started his blog. He made his blog the center of his social media efforts, and knew his writing would be the key element to having people become readers.

His editor is Kellie Bowers. You can see the value of her input from the results Sam has posted. Aside from quickly developing a large audience, Sam's posts during Blog Off II (these are weighted stats) brought him:

- ✓ 2540 page views for his posts
- ✓ An average reading time of 5 minutes, and
- ✓ 96 comments from readers

Sam started with the goal of providing useful content that is fun to read. To achieve that goal, he immediately "staffed a weakness" by choosing to work with an editor.

During Blog Off II, Sam made two posts. The first one was conversational. It focused on why LinkedIn and Twitter are small in comparison to Facebook. (Of course, there are also a few countries that are smaller than Facebook.)

The post generated a lot of comments, and Sam relied heavily on the comment roundup for replying. Read it at http://bit.ly/8XFF6A.

One of the things to keep in mind for any business activity is how much time it takes. You already know that spending two weeks planning and setting up an end-cap in a retail store is simply not going to return enough sales to justify the time and effort you've invested.

What makes social media harder to handle is that it can be so darned entertaining. There are thousands of interesting stories, videos and photos to look at – not to mention the posts and comments being made by everyone in your network.

Sam did an excellent job of answering specific comments and balancing the rest of his replies using comment roundups. This allowed him to "stay in the game" as far as general conversation was concerned, while focusing on the comments that allowed him to delve into specific issues.

Digging into those issues allows you, and Sam, to show the depth of your knowledge and expertise. It also gives your readers a reason to re-visit a particular post, and provides you with launching points for new posts.

Sam's second post was on the subject of Search Engine Optimization (SEO). Read the whole post at http://bit.ly/6qGxEN.

An interesting thing happened when Sam made this post – people got angry.

More than a few folks took exception to Sam suggesting that there is an ample supply of "SEO providers" who either don't know what they're doing, or are actively bamboozling their customers. The cool thing is that the controversy served to increase traffic to Sam's post.

Everyone seems to like a good argument.

To Sam's credit, he handled the disagreements with tact and his usual dash of humor.

It is almost inevitable that someone is going to disagree with something you write at some time. That's fine, and you want it to happen. Disagreement adds spice to the conversations, and it helps everyone look at an issue with a new perspective.

Which should also suggest to you that it isn't necessary to agree with every comment someone makes on your blog. When someone shows you where you've made a mistake, admit it, correct it and move on. Similarly, take the time to correct someone who leaves an incorrect comment.

When an issue centers on a difference of opinion, be tactful and make it clear that you respect the opinions of your readers. For occasions when it's a matter of contrasting or conflicting statistics, be sure you cite your sources.

Sam also gave Andrew a few comments that reflect his philosophy and passion for creating engaging content:

> We are amidst revolutionary times in the marketing world. In years past, "Branding" was for the big guys who had badgillions of dollars to throw into their marketing campaigns. However, as new technologies have emerged, scalability has become a paramount change. Today, the consumer has the ability to make their own "Personal Brand," and reach audiences that used to be off limits. And with a little creative juice, sometimes it's even possible for a personal brand to OUTMARKET those corporate players that used to control their niches by financial default.
>
> The key to building community is to interact with your readers through your content. Content writers seem to forget that there is an actual PERSON reading their copy. You can't just talk at people.... your content has to have a conversation with the reader. But even more importantly, you have to be able to grab those that didn't even know they wanted to read what you had to say. And then they have to be inspired to take an action eg. buy something, comment, etc. That is where viral marketing comes from. Try writing something controversial... see how powerful the result is.
>
> Throughout the contest, I found that simply reaching out to my fellow contestants had a tremendous impact on the relationships I made. Honestly, the big push came from creating gripping content. Unless you have something that creates discussion, you may see a few visitors, but they

won't tell their friends about it, and you won't see any result. The BEST referrers for traffic you can see are those that come from an e-mail box.

The question then becomes...how do you create discussion in your social media community?

Let's go back to the hardware store owner. Are you really going to create a heated discussion over whether to use GFI outlets (the kind with little circuit breakers in them) throughout a house?

You will if you have a lot of home renovators, electricians and do-it-yourselfers as customers.

What is your audience interested in? Since it's a hardware store, some of your audience might be particularly interested in the advantages of a zero clearance ceiling fan. Or maybe they have strong opinions on the merit of Scott's Turf Builder for their lawns.

Now let's go back to the idea of leveraging your audience to get participation. We covered this a little while discussing Sean Nelson's approach to Blog Off II.

You start with the people you know and get them involved in your social media community. Then you ask them to introduce other people to the community. This is all good stuff.

As you go along, you also want to consistently ask readers for their participation in the community. You know from personal experience that lots of people will just sit on the sidelines rather than jump in to participate. I'm sure you've seen people at countless networking events who just sit in a chair, or hover by the buffet table.

In the online world, it's even easier to visit a blog and read the content then leave without posting a comment. You have to ask for comments.

Of course, it doesn't have to be some canned phrase you use at the end of every post : "Hey, if you like what you've read then please leave a comment."

Yea. That's about as original and interesting as tuna straight from the can.

If you think Scott's Turf Builder is the best thing ever invented for growing a healthy, attractive lawn, then come out and say so – strongly. Give your reasons, and tell people where they can see lawns around town that are the result of using Scott's Turf Builder. You want to give people something they can disagree with.

Then follow Sam's example and reply to everyone's comment with respect, new information, and maybe even some humor.

Tim Ruffner (http://www.linkedin.com/in/timruffner)

Tim took a markedly different tack from Sean and Sam. He used a series of five posts, and his topic is not marketing.

Let me start by giving you the URLs to each of Tim's posts. They're listed in chronological order.

1. Bring Your Idea or Invention to Life http://bit.ly/5T2fQO
2. From Concept to Reality http://bit.ly/8E4lLy
3. 5 Steps to Patent Your Invention http://bit.ly/4HxjJc
4. Accelerate Your Product to the Market http://bit.ly/4rXpVG
5. 6 Steps to Manufacture Your Invention http://bit.ly/6tVRcR

Tim chose an evergreen topic – one that holds interest for generations and crosses normal audience divisions. Being able to choose an evergreen topic is always an advantage in getting people to read your material.

For example, almost everyone has an interest in retirement investing. Rich, poor, middle income, tradesmen, professionals, blue collar, white collar…retirement investing is a topic of interest to almost every audience.

Similarly, we all seem to have an interest in inventing the better mouse trap.

Writing posts in a series also adds loyalty to your audience. Once you have their interest, knowing that you're going to give them more information on the same topic keeps them coming back. That's why it's important for you to have specific goals for your social media efforts.

Let's go back to the hardware store owner. We'll say she lives in a town where gardening, gazebos and garage workshops are the big interests – everyone in town is involved with one or more of these hobbies.

The first thing you're going to do is set up a blog to write about each of these hobbies. But think about that for a second…

Do you set up three blogs? No. That's too much hassle.

You set up one blog with three categories

✓ Gardening
✓ Gazebos
✓ Garage Workshops

Then you can put articles (or posts) about each hobby under each category. For other, more static information – such as an online catalog, how-to articles, or customer stories – you can create a page for each element.

And keep in mind that you don't have to create all the content like Tim, Sam and Sean did. Find people in town who want to write about their hobbies and invite them to contribute.

Now you have your blog set up. Of course you have profiles on at least the Golden Trio sites, too. Hook your blog to each of those sites so you can notify all your contacts of new content whenever it's posted.

Now you have a way to communicate with everyone – your social media profiles. You also have a way to inform them – the blog. And information can travel in both directions. Growth is going to happen naturally as long as you're providing useful, relevant content.

Tim is a good example of this. He works for GPI Prototype and the posts he submitted relate directly to the services they provide. They build prototypes for their customers – including inventors.

Because his topic is evergreen, and his content is useful and relevant, Tim has terrific material for keeping his readers loyal and drawing in new readers.

What Tim is still a little lacking in is his audience. He's still a beginner with social media. As a result, his posts drew:

- ✓ 506 page views
- ✓ An average reading time of 3.35 minutes, and
- ✓ 47 comments

You can see from Tim's methodical, committed approach that it's only a matter of time before his audience grows. When it does, he'll also grow his social media community and business network.

Here's what Tim had to say about what he has learned from Blog Off II:

> *Social Media has enabled GPI's branding efforts by utilizing a few key websites; Twitter, LinkedIn, Facebook, Delicious, StumbleUpon and Youtube.*
>
> *I was able to establish camaraderie with fellow contestants by reading and commenting on each of their blogs. I made sure I added all the contestants to LinkedIn*

and Twitter to stay on top of their blog posts. I also asked them to read mine in return, however I found that most had already done that and gave me great feedback.

I was able to tap into my network of friends using myspace, facebook, linkedin and email. I strategically emailed those colleagues for each blog post I wrote.

Out of my 6 posts the one that generated the most hits was the one I was trying to market to my fellow colleagues who all know about rapid prototyping, the remaining 5 posts I tapped in to my friends and family for input on my writing skills before posting the main blog which pertained the most to New Product Development and my industry.

The Future of Blog Off

You know Andrew is going to continue building on his successes with the Blog Off competitions.

He currently plans to keep the competition running on a semi-annual basis. Whether it will remain open to all comers – and be divided according to skill level, or return to a marketing professionals venue hasn't been decided yet.

Do you have an opinion? Go ahead and give it to Andrew by visiting the Community Marketing Blog (www.communitymarketingblog. com). You can speak your peace by leaving a comment.

As I mentioned at the start of this chapter, one of the main functions for the Blog Off competition is to validate social media as a marketing tool. That means Andrew is going to continue measuring results and showing the world how to do it.

Andrew and I had a conversation on the telephone not too long ago. The main point of the whole conversation was that business owners are still playing about with social media. We need to get serious.

That means treating it like any other business venture and approaching social media with a plan. It means knowing what we want to achieve so we can measure whether we're getting it or not.

For example, someone recently told Andrew that he hadn't "monetized" the Blog Off competition because it didn't result in direct sales. Well, both Andrew and I think this particular fellow doesn't understand the value and power of social media from a public relations, thought leadership and branding perspective.

Andrew has increased the team supporting him in making the Blog Off competitions happen. His audience has increased to over 6 Million readers and viewers. He has had articles and white paper studies written about his event, and he has been asked to host an online Telesummit session for training on Super User LinkedIn Learning. (This invitation came within two weeks of Blog Off II ending.)

As a result of the foundation laid, Andrew now has more time to work on continuing the growth of the Blog Off Competition. He has corporate sponsors taking an interest, and he is getting global exposure. (Somebody tell me again how he hasn't "monetized" his efforts.)

Blog-Off II was not simply a test for the contestants but for Andrew himself. Social media is all about building a community and working with your peers to extend your reach and influence. But Andrew's own research shows that almost 90% of business owners are getting zero results from their social media efforts.

For Blog Off II to truly be a success, Andrew had to demonstrate that he could use social media to:

✓ Engage a team of his peers
✓ Connect with that extended audience to generate interest – in the form of more competitors and audience participation, and
✓ Reinforce his personal branding as a thought leader in social media marketing and strategic social media management

During 2009, Andrew put in over 2,000 hours of research and practical effort. He analyzed hundreds of social media sites and businesses to see what they were doing in social media.

As a result, Andrew identified 4 stages of social media progression.

✓ **Stage One** – the solo blogger who engages a community around them
✓ **Stage Two** –a community of writers working together to create content under one theme on one site such as Facebook, LinkedIn, or a blog with everyone bringing their community to that one central location
✓ **Stage Three** – working with key industry influencers and their communities to create media interest in the new community

you're building. (Andrew has used the Blog Off events as the hook for attracting media attention.)

✓ **Stage Four** – this stage is seen more often with large companies such as Kodak or Dell that have community engagement on sites like Flickr, Facebook, Twitter, the company's own blog/forum and more in a cohesive manner. The fourth stage is simply the third stage replicated several times over.

You can see how Blog Off II represented a test for Andrew to accomplish Stage Three of this growth process.

The results spoke for themselves as over 40 people became involved with the vision for Blog-Off II in just 3 weeks. The competition achieved over 27,700 page views, 110 posts, 1,262 new comments (which demonstrated not just volume but quality of engagement), and a page visit time of 2 to 6 minutes.

By the end the contest the blog site achieved a US site ranking at 22,381 and international ranking of 138,800 from Alexa.com.

Relationships have been formed within the community of 40+ participants at every level and new friendships and partnerships will extend beyond the Blog-Off event. The community Andrew and his team have built is poised at its tipping point.

My opinion is that Blog Off III will firmly place this community as an industry leader in demonstrating the practical, business use of social media and measuring results.

And an important part of that leadership is showing business owners that social media has far more similarities to the traditional marketing they are familiar with than it does differences. Yes, social media has more options and more bells & whistles, but the mystery surrounding social media is being artificially created by self-proclaimed gurus and pundits.

You can bet that

✓ Pete Cashmore is measuring results for Mashable
✓ Darren Rowse is measuring results for ProBlogger, and
✓ Amazon.com is measuring results, too

Do you want to measure how much your customers like you? There are already methods for measuring that, and they can be applied to social media. The gurus and pundits don't want business owners to know that because then the business owners would realise those gurus and pundits are fakes.

Strategic social media marketing requires many of the same skills as running a traditional, complex marketing campaign. It isn't a mystery, and there's no need to develop new methods of measurement.

What is needed is a professional group of marketers who understand their responsibility to get results in a new environment. It isn't the methods of measurement that need to change. They only need tweaking.

What has to change is the way marketers ply their trade. We have to demonstrate to you, the business owner, that we can get results for you in a social media environment. An environment that gives your customers far more power and control than they have ever had.

So the next time someone tells you it's hard to measure results from social media, stop and consider the example of Blog Off II. Then ask yourself this question:

Is my consultant telling me results are hard to measure because he or she doesn't know how to get results when using social media?

A quick way to find the answer to that question is to look at how much time and energy you were asked to invest in planning the social media marketing campaign. If your consultant just "walked in and started doing," then you need to find a professional.

A social media professional treats your entry into social media as though you are planning to open a store in a new market, or expand your product line to service a new market. We all know that takes time, planning and careful thought.

Social media is a new market – not simply a new tool.

For example, Morgan Stewart of MarketingProfs conducted a study during 2009. His team surveyed more than 2,300 consumers and interviewed almost 100 people on the street. Here's part of what he found:

> Among our findings was that 70% of consumers who visit Facebook at least once a month and are a "fan" of at least one company or brand don't believe they have given those companies permission to market to them. Moreover, 40% of those "fans" don't believe marketers are welcome in social networks at all.

When you look for a social media professional, ask them if they're aware of this study and what it means.

The Blog Off competitions are successful because they are giving participants what is desired – an opportunity to learn and grow, increased exposure, and valuable content (just to name three). Does your consultant understand that a social media campaign must be based on aligning with audience interests?

When your message is of interest to your audience, they have a positive experience. That makes them more interested in doing business with you, but it doesn't mean you can use social media to send marketing messages. Here's another bit of advice from Morgan Stewart:

> *Comparing data from this year with data collected in 2008, we see consumers' attitudes toward nonpermission (or "pushy") marketing messages souring fast. However, that isn't true for permission-based messages; consumers are very receptive to promotions and are reporting using coupons more often.*
>
> *In marketer-initiated communications, email is the preferred channel (75% of consumers overall), even among teens (64%) and college students (70%). Consumers prefer to maintain a church-and-state separation between how they communicate with friends and how they receive deals from the brands they follow.*

Your audience wants you to market to them. After all, they still have a need for your product or service. What they do not want is for "marketers" to invade their social media living room the way TV commercials do; not even when they're an avid fan and supporter.

Okay. I've gotten a little off topic, and done a bit of ranting. You can see I very much agree with Andrew, and am eager to do more toward weeding out the self-proclaimed experts. I'm also eager to keep learning from Andrew and the rest of the team.

For now, let's move on with the rest of the guide. The next chapter is about Social Bookmarking – as known as Social News Sites. As you read through the next chapter, give some thought to visiting Andrew's blog (www.communitymarketingblog.com) and bookmark it for yourself.

Then you'll be able to visit regularly.

7. Why Have Social Bookmarking?

Bookmarking has two fundamental aspects:
1. You bookmark web pages you like
2. You bookmark pages from your own site

The reason for bookmarking a page is to show the world – through the internet – that you like it. This is just one of the many ways you can give back to the online community.

As more and more visitors bookmark a page, it becomes increasingly popular and noticeable on the internet. Bookmarking tracks public opinion.

My preferred bookmarking services (I currently subscribe to 14) are Technorati and Delicious.

Technorati has a dynamite function called Twittorati that allows me to follow what is happening in the blogosphere. As general as that sounds, it's actually quite useful.

Technorati tracks everything that happens on the top 100 Blogs. I've gone through this list to find those blogs that are relevant to me. From that short-list, there are some I check on a regular basis (every other day). Everything else gets checked on weekends when I'm looking around to see what's happening in the world.

Of course, in addition to the top 100, Technorati tracks every other blog that's available (and getting traffic). Use the Search function to find blogs related to your keywords. Make a list of two or three dozen blogs that are relevant to your business. Then, once or twice a week, read the five most popular posts from the entire list.

This keeps you in touch with what's popular in your market and gives you ideas for you own e-zine or blog.

Let's review that quickly so it's clear.

Review the top 100 Blogs for those that are relevant to your market and review their content three or four times each week. Then, in addition to those blogs, make a list of two or three dozen other blogs that are relevant to you. Review this longer list just once or twice each week.

Be sure to avoid adding unnecessary blogs to your list because you think you might keep up on them. If a blog is not directly relevant to your business, then don't let it take up business time.

Delicious is a little more general than Technorati. It has an incredibly useful toolbar. (Unfortunately, Technorati doesn't have a toolbar – yet.)

The Delicious toolbar makes it possible for you to add a bookmark to your Delicious account every time you add a page to your browser's Favorites. Of course, it works in the other direction, too.

For example, you're visiting relatives in Istanbul and using their computer. You want to bookmark a site, so you login to Delicious and mark the site. When you get home, open your browser and login to Delicious. Their site allows you to update your browser's Favorites to include every bookmark you added during your trip.

But that's not all…

Every time you add a bookmark to Delicious, it gives you the opportunity to make notes about the page you're bookmarking. There are two fields: One for general notes about why you like the page and what you found useful. This is especially handy when you're bookmarking a page because it gave you an idea. The other field is for tags. The keywords you enter help other Delicious users to find the page you're bookmarking when they use the Delicious search function.

You can see how it's easy to end up with thousands of bookmarks. This is why I rely heavily on both Technorati and Delicious.

Just like favorites on your browser, you can organize bookmarks in Delicious using categories or folders. That makes Delicious ideal for bookmarking sites that are relevant to your market, a client or a specific project. Technorati is useful for bookmarking pages that aren't necessarily relevant to my business.

Of course, this still leaves the other 12 bookmarking sites to which I subscribe. What are they for?

The other sites help me do two things:

1. Spread some "link love"
2. Do research

When I find a blog post that is exceptional – it's filled with useful information or is insightful – I support the author by bookmarking the post on every bookmarking site I subscribe to. Unlike a trackback (when I link to someone's blog from my blog), the author doesn't get notified of bookmarks.

When I'm doing research for a new book, I visit the bookmarking sites to see what other people are looking at that's relevant to my topic.

Think of a bookmarking site as a vertical search engine. A typical search engine – Google or Yahoo – just looks everywhere for information about whatever you type into the search window. A bookmarking site only looks at the sites that have been bookmarked by other users like you and me.

You won't get the wide variety of material that a Google search digs up. What you do get is a list of sites discovered by people who have an interest in whatever topic you're looking at. I find things on the bookmarking sites that might be buried on page 83 or 200-and-something with a Google search.

Just keep in mind that they are two different tools. They overlap and complement each other, but one can never replace the other.

Now let's have a look at the bookmarking sites.

8.   The Social Bookmarking Sites

Site	Google	Alexa	Compete
http://www.technorati.com	9	676	535

Time Magazine says, "If Google is the Web's reference library, Technorati is becoming its coffee house."

Technorati enables you to collect and organize the blogs you want to follow. Technorati also offers a large array of widgets you can use on your blog and buttons for your browser.

A wonderful connection between Technorati and Twitter is called Twittorati. You can get there by going to http://twittorati.com.

Twittorati allows you to follow what's happening on Technorati's Top 100 Blogs, and they are planning to add many more of the web's most influential voices.

Technorati has a cool education report they publish each year titled *State of the Blogosphere*. This report shows you more than just the numbers indexed by Technorati. The report is a result of surveying bloggers directly to discover the tools they use, the impact (financial, social, and professional) blogging has had on their lives, and how they use blogging.

http://www.netscape.com	9	6,043	2,606

Provided by AOL.

Netscape allows you to keep track of all the web pages that interest you, connect with some social media networks (Twitter, Facebook. AIM, MySpace, and Bebo), and check several e-mail providers.

http://www.digg.com	8	156	18

Digg allows you to connect Digg with Facebook. This allows you to publish content from Digg onto your Facebook's wall and to transfer information about your friends onto Digg.

Think of Digg as a YouTube for blogs. The more attention your blog post gets, the more exposure you receive on Digg.

Digg has a toolbar, but you have to be logged in to see it. It isn't an add-on for any browser. The toolbar allows you to find related posts, find the source of a post, or bury the post all together.

Site	Google	Alexa	Compete
http://www.stumbleupon.com	8	417	291

Stumbleupon.com is elegantly different from all the other sites. This one is not about you putting information onto the internet. It's about you discovering new information on the internet.

You choose your interests – lifestyle, health, music, photos, whatever – and then click the stumble button. Stumbleupon.com takes you to web pages related to your interests. When you like what you find, you mark it with "I like this."

Simple, straightforward, and elegant, Stumbleupon.com is like backpacking across Europe without reservations.

http://www.reddit.com	8	664	269

Reddit describes itself in this way "Reddit is a source for what's new and popular online. Vote on links that you like or dislike and help decide what's popular, or submit your own!"

Reddit has a toolbar that can be added to Firefox. It displays when you click a link from Reddit – i.e. you have to be in Reddit to click the link. Then you can vote the article up or down using the toolbar.

They also have a widget that let's you get headlines from Reddit added to your site. They also offer buttons you can add to your site so people can bookmark your site using Reddit.

http://del.icio.us	8	704	4,267

Use www.delicious.com to access this bookmarking site.

Delicious has a toolbar you can download as an add-on to IE or Firefox. With the toolbar, you can instantly bookmark a site to Delicious and add it to your browser's list of favorites.

An interesting element of the Delicious site is the ability to search tags. (Tags are the keywords or key phrases people use to describe their posts.) So you can enter a tag and find blog posts that feature that tag.

Site	Google	Alexa	Compete
http://favorites.live.com	7	5	4

Provided by Microsoft. This site gives you 25GB to store your photos and files for sharing.

http://mystuff.ask.com	7	46	19

Ask.com enables you to search the internet for answers to questions. Although it takes you to web pages, it isn't the pages that Ask.com is indexing – it's the information, the answers to questions.

http://www.ilike.com	7	2,184	599

Targeted to music lovers.

http://www.diigo.com	7	3,287	8,552

A research and knowledge sharing tool. This site enables you to highlight and annotate information on web pages.

You can signup for a Diigo account or use your Google ID, Yahoo ID, or a MyOpenID to sign in to the site. As with most bookmarking sites, Diigo also has its own toolbar you can install as an add-on to your browser.

If you are a Furl user, you will have to do an account transfer before being able to sign in.

An interesting quirk to Diigo is that there is no obvious sign-out button. Just hover the cursor over your username at the top of the page (to the left of the search box). There is a drop-down menu that gives you access to Profile, Settings, Tools, and signing out.

Site	Google	Alexa	Compete
http://www.nowpublic.com	7	3,444	2,400

This site is a blog for everyone – it is a platform for citizen journalism.

Provided by NowPublic Technologies in Vancouver, BC (Canada), this site invites you to cover the news that's important to you and submit it to the blog.

http://www.newsvine.com	7	4,061	1,218

Newsvine is provided by MSNBC Interactive News.

Their objective is to cover the news and give the world a chance to comment on it.

http://www.mister-wong.com	7	6,624	22,320

This is a bookmarking site from Germany. You see this immediately when you visit the About page and find it written entirely in German. This site makes an interesting portal to other sites.

http://www.meneame.net	7	8,694	56,623

Are you looking for a social networking site in Spanish or Portuguese? This may be the site for you.

http://www.connotea.org	7	9,248	39,086

This is a reference management tool for clinicians and scientists.

They offer a unique tool that allows you to develop a bibliography with every bookmark you make. You can share those references or use them when compiling the bibliography for a new work.

http://www.citeulike.org	7	10,412	18,414

This site is similar to connotea.org. It is designed to allow you keep and sort references to other sources.

Site	Google	Alexa	Compete
http://www.rollyo.com	7	18,188	22,582

This site is in Beta.

Rollyo.com allows you to create your own search engine based on sources you know and trust. Essentially, you create a vertical search engine that looks only at the sites you tell it to look at.

http://www.jaiku.com	7	23,227	57,206

Jaiku is a part of Google. The service is maintained by volunteer Google engineers on their spare time.

This service seems quite similar to Twitter. The name "Jaiku" seems to be a play on the Japanese word "Haiku." Short poems have become short posts in the 21st century.

http://www.claimid.com	7	25,352	64,823

This is a site providing access to OpenID.

The concept of OpenID is that you can have access to multiple websites with just one user ID and password. Social networking sites, as well as stores (Sears and K-Mart), are using OpenID to make signing in easier.

http://www.yoono.com	7	34,745	0

This is an add-on for your Firefox or IE (in Beta) browser.

It allows you to stay connected to several social networking sites (including chat sites) at the same time.

http://www.rojo.com	7	1,114,778	174,191

Recently re-named to www.blogs.com.

This is a service similar to Technorati. It allows you to search other blogs for content.

Site	Google	Alexa	Compete
http://bookmarks.yahoo.com	6	2	2

A bookmarking service similar to Delicious.com. This one is, of course, provided by Yahoo.

Site	Google	Alexa	Compete
http://www.kaboodle.com	6	1,185	304

This is a bookmarking site for shoppers.

When you find a bargain, a new brand, good service – whatever – mark the site here and other shoppers will be able to find it.

Site	Google	Alexa	Compete
http://www.dzone.com	6	4,444	7,608

Targeted to developers and programmers.

This site will help you find that bit of code you've been looking for.

Site	Google	Alexa	Compete
http://www.stylehive.com	6	8,164	4,209

As you might guess from the name, this site aims to connect "stylish people" with each other.

Site	Google	Alexa	Compete
http://www.backflip.com	6	10,646	40,107

This site combines being able to find what's hot on the internet with building your own vertical search engine.

Site	Google	Alexa	Compete
http://www.bibsonomy.org	6	11,077	55,363

BibSonomy is offered by the Knowledge and Data Engineering Group of the University of Kassel, Germany.

This site is focused on literature.

Site	Google	Alexa	Compete
http://www.linkagogo.com	6	12,552	62,527

This is an online favorites manager and social bookmarking application.

They have three membership levels: free, plus and premium.

Site	Google	Alexa	Compete
http://www.simpy.com	6	14,921	36,419

Simpy is a social bookmarking service that lets you save, tag, search, and share your bookmarks, notes, groups, and more.

http://www.pligg.com	6	14,962	41,156

Similar to Ning – it allows you to create your own social networking community. The difference is that Pligg.com requires you to download software and use it on your site.

http://www.popurls.com	6	17,427	23,664

Popurls is the dashboard for the latest web-buzz; a single page that encapsulates up-to-the-minute headlines from the most popular sites on the internet.

http://www.netvouz.com	6	22,863	52,436

Netvouz is a social bookmarking service that allows you to save your favorite links online and access them from any computer, wherever you are.

http://www.bloghop.com	6	32,081	146,813

If you're searching for a blog, you can tagsurf to blogs that match your interest. If you're a blogger — add your blog here and make sure to include a good description.

This site does list adult content blogs in addition to all others.

http://www.kuro5hin.org	6	49,824	28,643

This is a site for people who want to discuss the world in which they live. It's a site for people who are on the ground in the modern world, and who sometimes look around and wonder what they have wrought.

Site	Google	Alexa	Compete
http://www.rawsugar.com	6	84,955	257,040

This may be a paid service. It's unclear on the homepage.
This site enables you to build your own vertical search engine.

http://www.nextaris.com	6	243,012	2,964,284

Your **all-in-one** toolkit for searching the Web, tracking news, capturing Web content, sharing files, publishing Web blogs, and private messaging.

http://www.wurldbook.com	6	257,963	3,584,200

Navigate, collect, categorize, annotate, clip, archive, find, publish RSS (including enclosures), and share information with others that is important to you on the web.

http://www.links2go.com	6	331,233	396,930

Links2go is a traditional Internet directory with a new twist on tags. You can search by topic or by keyword tag.

http://www.trexy.com	6	868,286	550,645

This site makes it possible for you to record the search path you take to find specific information. When you're searching for something new to you, you can check to see whether someone else on trexy.com has already developed a search path for that information.

http://www.hugg.com	6	3,164,008	308,359

Recently renamed to www.treehugger.com.
"Treehugger is the leading media outlet dedicated to driving sustainability mainstream. Partial to a modern aesthetic, we strive to be a one-stop shop for green news, solutions, and product information."

This is not a site you join the same way you join Facebook or LinkedIn. This site brings you information. They are providing you with bookmarks to find information of value to you.

Treehugger is currently #21 on Technorati's list of Top 100 Blogs.

Site	Google	Alexa	Compete
http://www.clipmarks.com	5	4,121	0

On Clipmarks.com, you can see clips of text, images, or video about all sorts of topics that other people find while surfing the web.

http://www.stylefeeder.com	5	7,092	2,262

As you add products from your favorite online stores, discover cool products added by other StyleFeeders, and rate products on a scale from 1 (hate it!) to 5 (love it!), this system is learning what you like.

http://www.corank.com	5	11,003	70,014

This site is in Beta.

You create web pages with content you like and let other people rate them.

http://www.searchles.com	5	12,510	29,411

This site allows you to build a vertical search engine to find information on only the sites you want to view.

http://www.spotback.com	5	13,005	56,891

Spotback is a personalized rating system that recommends relevant content based on personal rating history.

http://www.startaid.com	5	13,952	29,947

Startaid allows you to sort and categorize your bookmarks.

Site	Google	Alexa	Compete
http://www.mylinkvault.com	5	14,218	62,039

A service to organize your favorites that uses drag-and-drop technology to make it easier.

| http://www.buddymarks.com | 5 | 15,735 | 79,714 |

By default, your bookmarks are private, but when you choose to, you can share some or all of your bookmarks with a select group of friends (buddies, shall we say?). Or mark them as "Everybuddy," and you can share them with everyone.

| http://www.plime.com | 5 | 18,647 | 39,902 |

An editable wiki community where users can add and edit weird and interesting links.

| http://www.givealink.org | 5 | 23,278 | 240,527 |

Givealink is a social annotation, organization, recommendation, and navigation system for the web.

It is also a research project by the Networks and Agents Network in the Center for Complex Networks and Systems Research of the Indiana University School of Informatics. "The project is funded by National Science Foundation (award IIS-0811994: Social Integration of Semantic Annotation Networks for Web Applications)."

| http://www.wists.com | 5 | 24,530 | 22,307 |

This is a social shopping site.

| http://www.linkatopia.com | 5 | 39,418 | N/A |

Keep all your bookmarks in one place and decide which ones you would like to keep private and which can be public.

Site	Google	Alexa	Compete
http://de.lirio.us	5	39,646	11,852

This site plans to build a customized search engine for every ZIP Code in the US, that's over 40,000 search engines. Each one will promote websites that are either local or serve the area. This should give great results when looking for local services, information, or products.

http://www.myhq.com	5	41,080	59,357

Manage your bookmarks in a banner-ad FREE environment. Import/export, create public pages (password protected if you wish), and share bookmarks.

http://www.saveyourlinks.com	5	56,730	493,345

A web based bookmarking service that allows you to synchronize your bookmarks across different browsers and computers.

http://www.linkfilter.net	5	70,993	468,718

Each user has the ability to post links, vote on others' links, comment on links, chat, keep a journal, post a poll, and a bunch of other neat things. Everything you do earns you points. The more points you get, the more special features you can unlock.

http://www.gravee.com	5	77,024	331,629

This site enables you to connect with other bookmarking sites to keep everything in order and to connect with Facebook and MySpace.

http://www.voo2do.com	5	90,914	N/A

Looking for a service to help you coordinate all your social media projects? This may be the site that helps you get the job done.

Site	Google	Alexa	Compete
http://www.carnatic.com	5	394,957	810,650

Interested in Carnatic music? That's the classical music of Southern India. Then this is the site for you.

http://www.fark.com	4	3,089	N/A

A news aggregator and an edited social networking news site. Two membership levels: free and TotalFark ($5/month)

http://www.bluedot.us	4	6,543	473,120

Recently renamed to www.faves.com
In addition to seeing bookmarks from your friends, you can subscribe to topics on Faves.com to see all the newest content about the topics you care about.

http://www.oyax.com	4	11,685	54,796

Allows you to add web sites to your personal collection of links, categorize those sites with tags, and share your collection not only with your own browsers and machine, but also with other people.

http://www.a1-webmarks.com	4	11,748	60,118

This is a complete service for indexing, sorting, and validating your bookmarks. On this site, they're called webmarks.
This site also allows you to share your bookmarks publicly and search the public bookmarks of other users.

http://ww2.ikeepbookmarks.com	4	17,908	55,677

Allows you to upload and keep your bookmarks on the web for free. You can also mark your bookmarks as private or public.

Site	Google	Alexa	Compete
http://www.sitejot.com	4	24,657	200,630

Allows you to store all your bookmarks/favorites in one online location, making them easy to access and manage from anywhere.

http://www.blogmarks.net	4	26,536	55,139

Organize and access your bookmarks from any computer. Share them with other internet users.

http://www.getboo.com	4	27,153	163,896

This service offers the unique ability to make some bookmarks private and leave others public. Useful for sharing resources among group members and keeping them private.

http://www.maple.nu	4	28,188	457,237

A generic bookmarking site.

http://www.linkroll.com	4	28,737	18,473

Bookmark, categorize, and comment on all the great web pages/ links you find.

Browse other users' bookmarks, and subscribe to users and link categories that appeal to you.

http://www.bookkit.com	4	38,910	401,378

A free service to sort, synchronize, and manage your bookmarks.

http://www.tagtooga.com	4	39,690	49,972

This is an online directory of bookmarks that anyone can edit.

Site	Google	Alexa	Compete
http://www.sync2it.com	4	44,909	54,926

This is an application you download and install on your computer to keep bookmarks synchronized across multiple browsers and computers.

http://www.chipmark.com	4	54,560	233,602

Get your bookmarks from any computer, anywhere, whether you're at home, work, a library, or at school.

http://www.feedmarker.com	4	69,674	170,389

Feedmarker lets you bookmark items from the Web and read RSS and Atom feeds. It also lets you organize all your feeds and marks using an open tagging system.

http://www.ifaves.com	4	71,731	1,044,354

A bookmarking service that helps you organize and prioritize your favorites.

http://www.jeteye.com	4	96,859	167,008

This service enables you to create libraries of your bookmarks and call them Jetpaks.

http://www.butterflyproject.nl	4	162,171	987,950

You can add hyperlinks and notes, highlight words, look up information, translate selections, and more.

http://thumblicio.us	4	472,727	1,374,852

Thumblicious is a new way to browse the internet, by displaying screenshots of the most popular sites from del.icio.us.

Site	Google	Alexa	Compete
http://www.yattle.com	3	24,395	260,974
http://www.wobblog.com	3	24,755	173,098
http://www.aboogy.com	3	25,463	463,418
http://www.ambedo.com	3	101,533	646,596
http://www.thinkpocket.com	3	113,291	643,178
http://www.reader2.com	3	213,316	311,035

Similar to LibraryThing.com. Just a little less functionality.

http://www.rrove.com	3	239,305	N/A
http://www.tutorialism.com	3	338,662	758,476
http://www.feedalley.com	3	503,962	0
http://www.ez4u.net	2	46,503	1,441,931
http://www.i89.us	2	78,212	887,630
http://www.allmyfavorites.net	2	81,604	405,409
http://www.myprogs.net	2	185,206	1,163,261

The only site I've seen dedicated to people telling each other about their experiences using different software.

http://www.tabmarks.com	2	205,952	1,953,844
http://dev.upian.com/hotlinks/	1	306,548	396,976
http://www.recipe-buzz.com	1	1,084,252	4,332,235
http://www.cloudytags.com	0	20,519	237,280
http://www.aworldofhelp.com	0	270,158	3,572,812
http://www.connectedy.com	???	31,851	104,538

9. What is Video Sharing?

We've all heard of YouTube. If your friends are like mine, you probably get one or two e-mails every week sending you to the latest YouTube video of somebody doing something wild and zany.

Basically, *video sharing* is putting a video onto any site other than your own. When you put a video on your own site, it's probably directly related to your business.

Something I should point out right away is that a lot of sites allow you to share video that aren't listed in this section. For example, Facebook and Bebo allow you to share video and aren't listed here. On other social media sites, video is something they've added to increase the attractiveness of their service.

The sites listed in this section are here because video is their primary reason for existing.

Some of these sites are, like Facebook and Bebo, services you can easily use to share, store and organize videos you want to share with family and friends. And, just like other sites, you can use them to promote your business. Then there are sites such as Vimeo and Viddler.

These are sites designed for use by business owners. You'll definitely want to pay attention to the video sharing sites that cater to business owners before spending time on CollegeHumor.com.

I'll tell you about some resources you can put to use for learning about video, and how to use it for promoting your business, in this chapter. First, though, we should start with some basics about:

✓ What you can do with video
✓ What equipment you need, and
✓ Video formats

Obviously there is far more content covered by those headings than I can reasonably cover in just one chapter. To help you be well prepared for using video, I'll mention a couple of resources directly in this chapter, and there is a whole appendix with resources (free and paid) you can explore: Appendix C – Video Resources.

What You Can Do With Video

Here are four ways you can use video to promote your business:

1. Screen Capture Videos
2. PowerPoint Videos (PPT Videos)
3. Animation/Lecture Videos
4. Talking Head Videos

Whichever type of video you decide to make, be sure to spend some time planning it.

As with any other project, you'll save time and effort by having a clear plan of what you want to accomplish and what you're going to do. In the case of video, that means putting together a script and making sure you have all your props ready.

When you make a screen capture video, make sure you have all the programs or websites you need ready to go. Every video needs some notes about what you will say while recording, and you're going to take notes while you're recording the video, too.

Expect to stop and start the video several times while you're recording. You might want to change locations, re-shoot something, or change your props around. Whatever the reason, be sure to note what you were saying and where things were when you stopped the camera.

It could look really strange to have something jump from your left hand to right hand during the video. Then again, that might be just the quirk you need to make your video original and attention-getting.

Screen Capture Videos

Frank Kern and Trey Smith use this type of video in their *Screw Google* video series.

It works well because they need to show customers how to fill in forms on various sites, and how to use different functions within Clickbank, Yahoo Search Marketing and Tracking 202. A screen capture video literally records what they are doing on the screen while recording their narration.

A lot of service sites (Aweber, 1ShoppingCart) use this type of video to show you how to get started on their site.

It's an extremely effective method because it combines visual and auditory learning. With the pause button, you can also incorporate physical learning by stopping the video and doing what you've been shown. Personally, I'm a big fan of this video style. There have been dozens of times when I've benefited from it simply because I've been able to rewind, watch what someone does, then go to my own web page and do it myself.

Camstudio is just one program that lets you make screen capture videos. It's free, and I can tell you from personal experience that it is completely easy to use. You just start the program, hit the record button, and do whatever you want to demonstrate.

PowerPoint Videos

This is an incredibly simple form of video to produce that fits in well with the other three types.

You've probably seen a PowerPoint presentation – maybe even more of them than you'd like to remember. But one of the great things about PowerPoint is that you can set the slide show to run automatically.

When it comes to making a video, you might set up a few slides to run automatically while you narrate. Then you can use a talking head or screen capture video to elaborate on one or more points from those slides.

Of course, a PowerPoint Video is the first cousin to an animation/ lecture video. The reason they're separated here is that PowerPoint offers you its whole package of tools for creating your presentation.

Animation/Lecture Video

You've already seen an example of this kind of video in Chapter 2 – What is Social Networking. It's the video from Lee LeFever that's mentioned at the end of the chapter.

Lee uses some cool paper animations combined with his lecture to show people like you and me how things work. His site is www. CommonCraft.com. You should definitely visit his site as a learning resource, and his videos are strong examples for you to emulate.

Talking Head Videos

This is the kind of video we all see on landing pages everywhere.

It's usually shorter than 5 minutes, and it's just a person – shown from the chest up – talking about whatever is featured on the landing page. One of the reasons these videos are short is that watching a talking head is boring.

On the other hand, using this video form for testimonials is truly effective. Keep the testimonial short – less than a minute, and less than 30 seconds if possible.

You can always support the video by having a text version of the testimonial with it.

This is not, by any means, an exhaustive list of the way you can make videos to promote your business. These are the most popular methods, and you can combine them, make up your own method, or just surf YouTube to see examples of all kinds of video forms.

The main thing to keep in mind when you're choosing a video form is what you want the video to do.

A video you're putting on your site is the easiest because it has the whole site to support it and give the video context. Even a slightly boring talking head video can be effective when it makes something easier for visitors to your site.

Videos for landing pages are slightly harder than site videos. When people hit a landing page, they know they're being sold so your video needs to grab their attention. Whichever form you use, it certainly can't be boring or hard to understand. Ideally, it should also be fairly short – almost never longer than 5 minutes.

Of course, neither of these is quite as special as a video you want to put onto one of the video sharing sites.

When you put a video on YouTube, Viddler or Multiply, it doesn't have any of the context supports that come with putting a video on your site or a landing page. The video has to accomplish its mission all by itself. Fortunately, there are a few easy tweaks you can make to any video before sharing it.

The first thing you can tweak is the opening scene of your video. Make sure it introduces you and the reason for the video.

Just as a sales letter opens with an attention getting headline, give one to your video, too.

The point is to give viewers a reason to keep viewing.

A second tweak is to make sure the video ends with a strong call to action. When you're taking a video from your landing page, it probably already has this. But a video on your website might not need a call to action beyond asking visitors to read the text on the page.

When it's on a video sharing site, your video has to "close the sale" all by itself.

And that leads to the third tweak. Be sure to include your URL (website address), telephone number, or whatever else it is you're giving people as a means of taking action.

When you're asking someone to visit your website, it makes sense to tell them what the address is, yes?

There are other things you can do to tailor your video for use on a video sharing site. A good place to start learning about video production and how to use video is www.makeinternettv.org.

These folks cover everything from equipment and shooting video all the way through to publishing and promoting your video. The best thing about this site is that anyone – at any skill level – can go there and get useful information. Another cool thing is that the site is free.

Another good resource – but this one isn't free – is a book by John Moreau titled _Online Video – A Step by Step Guide_. I'm mentioning this book because makeinternettv.org is all about how to make a video and promote it. That's good, but John's book is specifically about using video to improve conversion rates on landing pages and how to use clips from your video to generate traffic.

There are just a couple more things to cover before we move on to look at the video sharing sites.

One of those things is the equipment you need to make a video.

You already know I'm not any kind of professional cameraman or film maker, so I'm not going to try to tell you about which cameras are best. What I can tell you is that I've used a Sony Cybershot – just a little pocket camera – to shoot video and it turned out just fine.

When I needed to edit it, I used Nero to do it. That was because Nero was the only software I had – that I knew about – that could do the editing. As it turns out, your machine probably already has Windows Movie Maker on it, and that will edit your video, too. (Mine did – I just didn't know about it until this year.)

Miller Goodman, a friend who is a professional film maker – and who definitely knows cameras, lighting, and everything else about filmmaking – also gave me some advice about cameras. We were in Texas shooting a DVD series, and Miller told me about the cameras he was using.

He used handheld digital video cameras. What I mean is that they were small – he actually used tripods and a cool boom apparatus. He told me two of the cameras were less than $300, and that he was getting as good results from his digital cameras as he could get from bigger equipment he used to use.

My point is that you don't have to spend a fortune, or be a techno-wizard to make a video. Heck, when I made my first videos, my "tripod" was a 2" D-ring binder and my "set" was the meeting room in a friend's condo building. I've even seen a video from Rich Schefren that he shot sitting on the beach.

The other thing to mention is video format. Miller told me there are literally hundreds of formats available for video, and that can be a real pain in the neck.

On the bright side, there are 6 formats that are commonly used on the internet and one of them works just about everywhere – even on both Macs and PCs. Here are the formats:

1. AVI (.avi) – it stands for Audio Video Interleave (whatever that means) and most Windows computers can play it because the format was developed by Microsoft.

2. Windows Media Format (.wmv) – this is a common format, but it does require an extra bit of software before you can play it. The software is free, but needing it makes this format un-playable for anyone not using Windows.

3. MPEG (Moving Pictures Expert Group) (.mpg or .mpeg) – this format is very popular on the internet. It also comes in .mp2 and .mp4. MP3, of course, is the audio version of this file type.

4. QuickTime (.mov) – you've probably heard of QuickTime Player. Some sites tell you this software is needed before you can play the videos on that site. The software is free, and it lets you play DVDs on your computer, too.

5. RealVideo (.rm or .ram) – this one is similar to QuickTime, only it was developed by Real Player. It's useful for streaming video and internet TV, but you do need the player installed on your computer. The basic Real Player software is free.

6. Shockwave (.swf) – this one is better known as Flash Video. Flash players are free, and this is far and away the most popular form of video on the internet. That's partly because this format is playable by just about everyone – Mac or PC, Windows or non-Windows – and it works for landing pages, websites, video sharing and even those annoying little animations that "flash" at you from some websites.

The last thing to mention is a reminder to look at Appendix C – Video Resources.

There are lots of sites for you to visit, bits of software to look at, and guides to download. A couple of them have prices attached, but I've tried to find as many resources as possible that are free. If you know of any that I missed, please send me an e-mail at feedback@theconradhall. com. Put "video resources" in the subject line so I know why you're writing, and I'll gladly add the resource to the guide for next year.

And I'll mention your name as the person who told me about it, too.

10. The Video Sharing Sites

Site	Google	Alexa	Compete
http://www.youtube.com	9	3	7

Provided by Google.

YouTube allows people to easily upload and share video clips on www.YouTube.com and across the Internet through websites, mobile devices, blogs, and email.

http://vids.myspace.com	8	11	10

The MySpace.com networking site gives you groups and friends to participate with. Take that concept and add the use of video.

This site is part of MySpace.com. Using this link allows you to access it directly. You can sign in to MySpace.com from here and access all the other functions.

http://www.vimeo.com	8	464	427

Targeted specifically to videographers. This site offers two membership levels: free and Plus ($59.95/yr).

The upgraded membership gives you access to tools for publishing your videos.

http://www.ustream.tv	8	842	1,531

This site allows you to broadcast your own show to the internet. You can, if you want, be live 24 hours a day.

The site allows viewers to comment on your broadcast – you can also use the chat area to do Q&A sessions with viewers. The chat area has a second function that allows viewers to chat with their friends – who are not currently watching – through Twitter.

Site	Google	Alexa	Compete
http://www.getmiro.com	8	32,747	45,063

Miro is free software you download to your computer.

It allows you to play any video format (including HD), and it enables you to publish video, too. You can even put a Feed button on your site with Miro so visitors can subscribe to receive new videos automatically.

Miro is provided by a nonprofit organization creating a level playing field to enable everyone to reach large audiences with their content.

http://video.google.com	7	1	1

This is not truly a video sharing site, but it's worth mentioning.

As with other content on Google, this site shows videos based on popularity. Searching through the videos here can show you what is popular and give you ideas. It's also a nice place to visit when one of your videos gets popular.

http://video.yahoo.com	7	2	2

Yahoo allows you to upload video, review videos, and watch videos.

Interestingly, Yahoo is the only large video site that suggests creating content for your site by collecting videos and displaying them; edited as a collage or as is.

http://video.msn.com	7	6	5

This site allows you to upload, rate, and watch videos.

http://video.aol.com	7	33	11

This site does not do its own uploads. AOL uses Motionbox to upload videos to its site. Everything else is through AOL.

Site	Google	Alexa	Compete
http://www.dailymotion.com	7	71	280

Dailymotion is about finding new ways to see, share, and engage your world through the power of online video. You can find and upload videos about your interests and hobbies, eyewitness accounts of recent news and distant places, and everything else from the strange to the spectacular.

http://www.metacafe.com	7	135	244

This site specializes in short-form video content. Their average video length is 90 seconds.

To be posted to the site, your video must be approved through a community audition.

http://www.tinypic.com	7	164	343

A fast, simple, and reliable video and image hosting site that you can use to share your experiences. There is no registration or log-in required, simply submit your picture or video.

You upload your video or image and they provide you with a simple URL (e.g. http://tinypic.com/1) that is guaranteed to be unique. It will point to only your video or image. You can then copy and paste the link they provide to share your pictures on your favorite sites all without having to upload your image or video all over again.

http://www.multiply.com	7	183	1,491

This site offers photo and video sharing aimed at families. Multiply provides a wide range of privacy options for the content you upload. (It's also listed in the Social Networking Section.)

In addition to online sharing, it provides functions for producing print products (calendars, photo books, cards, etc.). This site is well worth checking out if you are into sharing photos and/or videos with friends and family.

Site	Google	Alexa	Compete
http://www.veoh.com	7	207	293

This site offers videos to watch and comment on, plus it has a browser plug-in that lets you download videos and organize them in a library. There is also a browser add-on that recommends related videos while you surf.

http://www.break.com	7	421	377

Break.com targets men age 18 to 34.

http://www.webshots.com	7	463	265

This site is focused on photos and videos. They offer two membership levels: free and premium (no price given).

You can use this site to create photo products such as prints, mugs, mouse pads, etc. They also have a downloadable photo application that allows you to interact more easily with Webshots.com.

http://www.collegehumor.com	7	1,506	1,282

Focus at collegehumor.com is on college students, but open to everyone.

This is one of the few sites that generates its own content. Several times each week, they record comedy videos and publish them on the site.

http://www.blip.tv	7	2,147	1,467

Focused on entrepreneurs, this site offers a place to actively develop and promote a TV- quality show.

http://www.funnyordie.com	7	2,813	1,763

This site has both user-generated and original content. It provides a place where people who produce funny content can test what they've done.

The site has a voting process in place that enables you to have feedback on what you've produced. It's a good place to test new videos to make sure you're on target.

Site	Google	Alexa	Compete
http://www.videojug.com	7	3,018	2,643

This site produces professional, how-to videos. They research and produce the videos, so they could make a good JV partner.

This is not a site where you can upload a video you have made.

http://www.brightcove.com	7	5,208	325

This is a paid service.

It is an online video platform you can use when you're ready to move from "home movie" quality to professionally produced video.

http://www.atomfilms.com	7	6,202	36,047

Provided by MTV Entertainment.

They are giving amateurs a "place to go pro." This is a place for comedic talent to test new material and develop a reputation.

http://www.current.tv	7	2,724,180	250,675

This is an internet-based television network. They have won an Emmy Award and target young adults.

They pay for some content, and allow you to post other content for which they do not pay.

http://www.lulu.tv	7	7,826,522	0

This is the same company that offers book publishing services.

In the same way they provide fulfillment for book publishing, they help you to sell your CDs and DVDs.

Site	Google	Alexa	Compete
http://www.megavideo.com	6	74	825

One of the few blatantly commercial video sites.

You must be a member to upload video content and you keep 100% of advertising revenues generated.

Memberships are offered for one or three months and one or two years. There is also a lifetime membership offered for a one-time fee of $199.99.

Site	Google	Alexa	Compete
http://www.4shared.com	6	95	2,581

This site is basically an online storage facility. They offer two membership levels: free and paid.

There are several subscription options from five days up to one year.

Site	Google	Alexa	Compete
http://www.esnips.com	6	859	4,448

Offers no restrictions on what you are allowed to upload and share.

They have a complete array of privacy options to help you share only with the people you choose.

Site	Google	Alexa	Compete
http://www.blinkx.com	6	1,316	1,367

You can upload content to this site, but you may find it more useful as a research tool. They are connected with several mainstream media outlets. That means you can research news broadcasts and other media.

Site	Google	Alexa	Compete
http://www.liveleak.com	6	1,541	2,721

This site has adult content on the homepage.

It provides user-generated content. LiveLeak.com is experiencing growing pains. The developer of the site, LL Hayden, posted an update on July 28, 2009 to update users.

Site	Google	Alexa	Compete
http://www.sevenload.com	6	1,601	13,639

Targeting photos and video, this site offers a venue for broadcasting your internet TV show.

http://www.ebaumsworld.com	6	1,828	1,511

Offers a platform to upload your video content. They cover most topics and accept video, photos, animation, etc.

http://www.livevideo.com	6	2,073	2,049

A platform for uploading your videos or developing an internet TV show.

http://www.revver.com	6	2,312	2,379

Share your videos here and share in the advertising revenue.

http://www.viddler.com	6	2,593	2,509

This site is set up to grow with you as you develop your business. You can start with their free service, and then apply for their Professional Video Publishing program.

The pro program allows you to share in ad revenues.

Finally, you can subscribe ($100/month) to their business package for developing video products.

http://www.heavy.com	6	2,904	735

Targeting video entertainment for men.

http://www.expertvillage.com	6	4,607	1,310

This site has been re-named to www.eHow.com.

Without the limitation of 5min.com, you can upload a teaching video to this site. There is also a program that enables you to generate revenue from your videos.

Site	Google	Alexa	Compete
http://www.jokeroo.com	6	5,046	12,187

Comedic content is featured on this site.

| http://www.jibjab.com | 6 | 5,339 | 1,555 |

Looking for an e-card for that perfect occasion? You'll probably find it here.

| http://www.i-am-bored.com | 6 | 5,718 | 5,356 |

A site devoted to alleviating your boredom using video.

| http://www.guba.com | 6 | 6,268 | 8,598 |

A general site for sharing video.

| http://www.gorillamask.net | 6 | 6,719 | 7,102 |

This site contains adult content.
A general site for any and all video content.

| http://www.blogtv.com | 6 | 7,082 | 14,659 |

As the name implies, this is a site where you can broadcast your internet TV show.

| www.stupidvideos.com | 6 | 13,159 | 10,214 |

There's a lot more content here than the name implies. Still, the site is strictly for entertainment.

| www.stupidvideos.com | 6 | 13,159 | 10,214 |

This is the site AOL uses for uploading video to its site.
They give you unlimited file storage, editing tools, and full-screen HD playback (assuming your video is in HD).

Site	Google	Alexa	Compete
http://www.motionbox.com	6	18,290	20,811

This is a UK based service.

A website and TV channel that showcases the best in User Generated Content. This site shares the revenue earned from user submissions with the people who actually make the content.

http://www.sumo.tv	6	18,468	14,597

This is an internet TV platform with high-quality production. You can't just post your content – you have to be good enough to be accepted.

http://tv.oneworld.net	6	38,064	58,207

Tv.oneworld.net targets audiences interested in ecology and the environment.

There is good content on this site. You are welcome to contribute and share relevant videos.

http://www.babelgum.com	6	19,489	6,058

A free, revolutionary Internet and Mobile TV platform supported by advertising, Babelgum combines the full-screen video quality of traditional television with the interactive capabilities of the Internet and offers professionally produced programming on-demand to a global audience.

http://www.teachertube.com	6	48,898	20,964

An online community for sharing instructional videos.

They seek to fill a need for a more educationally focused and safe venue for teachers, schools, and home learners. It is a site to provide easily accessed professional development with teachers teaching teachers.

It is a site where teachers can post videos designed for students to view in order to learn a concept or skill.

Site	Google	Alexa	Compete
http://www.ourmedia.org	6	60,639	30,437

A community of individuals dedicated to spreading grassroots creativity through videos, podcasts, and other works of personal media.

| http://www.showmedo.com | 6 | 64,732 | 105,303 |

Showmedo is an instructional site utilizing (Free and) Open-source software (FOSS). "We were inspired to start Showmedo by watching some very effective web video-tutorials/screencasts. These convinced us that web-videos can be a great way to quickly and efficiently acquire knowledge. It can even be fun, or at least painless. For some things there is no substitute to seeing it done."

| http://www.sutree.com | 6 | 68,703 | 40,715 |

This is a site for how-to videos.
The content covers everything from how to give a massage to how to select a yo-yo.

| http://jaycut.com | 6 | 131,624 | 165,252 |

This site is in Beta.
This site is targeting people who need to edit their video. You can upload and share your video, but the focus is on giving you a free tool to edit, mix, and publish video content.

| http://www.freevlog.org | 6 | 243,505 | 599,660 |

A site for video blogging. Instead of typing your blog entry, you record the entry as a video.

| http://www.viewdo.com | 6 | 292,652 | 106,898 |

A site for how-to videos.

Site	Google	Alexa	Compete
http://www.twango.com	6	649,905	558,272

A simple, clean site with unlimited storage for your photos and videos.

http://www.yourfilehost.com	5	126	3,478

This site contains adult content.
Upload and share any content anonymously.

http://www.mefeedia.com	5	1,662	1,600

This site allows you to connect to your YouTube, Blip, DailyMotion, or Vimeo accounts.
This is a good, smooth site with lots of groups for interaction.

http://www.vidivodo.com	5	4,088	38,407

A site for producing and broadcasting your own internet TV show.

http://www.funnyjunk.com	5	4,332	4,277

The name says it all for this site. Videos that are supposed to be funny – and some are – but mostly junk.

http://www.5min.com	5	5,147	2,173

If you can teach how to do something in five minutes or less, then your video qualifies for this site.
You must teach how to do something – that's important.
The site is free, and offers a lot of advice and instruction to make your content attractive to viewers.

Site	Google	Alexa	Compete
http://www.flixya.com	5	6,381	13,242

This site uses Google Adsense to enable users to generate revenue. They accept most content, and it's free to join.

| http://www.dailyhaha.com | 5 | 17,711 | 13,647 |

Pictures, videos, games and jokes. All comedic content.

| http://www.expotv.com | 5 | 17,904 | N/A |

Targets online shoppers and helps them share their bargain finds.

| http://www.onetruemedia.com | 5 | 19,486 | 10,066 |

This site helps families edit and share their videos.

There are two membership levels: free and premium ($3.99/month or $39.99/yr). This is a site well worth visiting to produce videos if you're not good with other software.

| http://www.vidmax.com | 5 | 20,502 | 20,241 |

This is a site for the more extreme videos.

You will see content of people being injured.

| http://www.kaneva.com | 5 | 33,011 | 29,274 |

A 3D interactive location for socializing.

This site requires you to download and install software.

| http://www.funnyhub.com | 5 | 33,399 | 22,289 |

Presents comedic content.

Site	Google	Alexa	Compete
http://www.yourdailymedia.com	5	39,806	30,269

A smaller site for submitting and viewing video and animation.

http://www.dropshots.com	5	47,055	24,479

An excellent site for sharing photos and video. You can automatically update other networking sites: Facebook, MySpace, Blogger, Friendster, etc.

This site does NOT make your content available for indexing or searching automatically. You must choose to make your content public. Most sites are set the other way.

You can even password protect any, or all, of your content as well as generate custom materials such as mugs, calendars, photo prints, etc.

http://www.zooppa.com	5	55,101	180,484

This site provides users an opportunity to develop advertising for companies such as Google and ING. The company provides a creative brief, and you develop an ad using any media you think suitable.

The ads are voted on by the community. Winners are eligible to receive a monetary prize.

http://www.sclipo.com	5	55,772	100,787

Sclipo is a social learning network. Sclipo helps people learn and teach better through eLearning apps (course manager, doc & video library, webcam-based classroom for live teaching, a live meeting room for tutoring) integrated with social features.

There are two levels of membership: free and premium ($6.95/month). A premium membership allows you to provide fee-based classes and get paid by students. Otherwise, the content on this site is provided free.

Site	Google	Alexa	Compete
http://www.dumpalink.com	5	55,796	52,398

This site has adult content on the homepage.
It is a general site for video.

http://www.yikers.com	5	60,500	40,798

This is a general site for posting videos, photos, and jokes.

http://www.clipshack.com	5	67,600	107,150

The mission of ClipShack is to be the easiest, most fun site for sharing and playing with video.

http://www.funnyplace.org	5	83,995	107,112

Focused on comedic content.

http://www.spymac.com	5	91,505	732,089

This site offers monetary incentive for being voted "the best" on their site.
The site is provided internationally, so it gives you a lot of planned, deliberate coverage for your content.

http://www.tagworld.com	5	117,667	141,113

This is a French site for photographers and videographers.
The homepage lists several contests for artists.

http://www.holylemon.com	5	146,722	120,244

Focused on comedic content.
If you're thinking this phrase looks pasted into place for some of these sites, it's because you can only stand so much comedy in a day. When you want your video to stand out, try to come up with something better than just being funny.

Site	Google	Alexa	Compete
http://www.dorks.com	5	156,246	99,095

A general video site for content suitable for ages 14 and up.

http://www.clipblast.com	5	252,137	119,359

A free service to watch and provide videos.

They have several tools for content creators to increase traffic to their sites and videos. This site is worth a visit.

http://engagemedia.org	5	364,584	460,870

EngageMedia is a video sharing site about social justice and environmental issues in the Asian Pacific.

http://www.hictu.com	5	608,443	1,048,318

A video blogging service that allows you to post content on any topic.

http://www.thedailyreel.com	5	2,785,001	2,057,961

A site for video blogs.

The most recent content seems to be from March '09.

http://www.scenemaker.net	5	13,014,163	1,675,384

This site is for people with lots of video content to manage. They provide fee based services to help manage video content.

www.flurl.com	4	1,886	7,658

This site allows you to upload and search videos. It indexes video from several other sites such as YouTube, Revver and DailyMotion.

It also provides a toolbar to make using the site easier.

Site	Google	Alexa	Compete
http://www.mojoflix.com	4	9,761	30,810

This is an adult oriented site for video.

http://www.vidiac.com	4	23,529	50,872

This site is provided by magnify.net.

Magnify.net is a video publishing platform that makes it easy for you to integrate user-generated video, video that you produce, or video that you discover into your website. It allows: uploading, sharing, creating playlists, making comments, reviewing, easy design templates, content controls, site reporting, help forums, and monetization options.

http://www.guzer.com	4	35,827	17,955

This is a general site for funny videos and photos.

http://www.tubetorial.com	4	42,318	73,958

This site specializes in videos that show you how to do things. In particular, this site provides "how to" videos to help you develop your online business.

This is a simple site for watching videos. A quirk with this site is that the About page seems to be blank.

http://www.videovat.com	4	58,048	31,641

This site is targeted to providing information and knowledge to users. Entertainment is not part of the purpose of this site.

You can upload almost any media form – in addition to video – and the media you upload can contain links to take users to a purchase area.

Site	Google	Alexa	Compete
http://www.myvideo.co.za	4	96,846	706,561

Personal video service focused on offering the best quality in video, privacy control, and overall ease of use. Videos you post to the site are NOT automatically available to the public.

http://www.freeiq.com	4	119,281	150,934

This site is specifically designed to allow you to share digital media on the internet and through your mobile phone.

http://www.viddyou.com	4	120,699	201,098

This is a video blogging site.

http://www.treemo.com	4	129,733	172,425

Treemo is an online and mobile community dedicated to sharing digital media. Share your photos, videos, and text.
This site is in Beta.

http://www.dailycomedy.com	4	277,861	108,706

All comedy, all the time. This site allows you to submit, watch, and rate comedy videos from around the world.

http://www.flukiest.com	4	286,663	473,281

Share your life with friends and the rest of the world. Make new friends or connect with old ones from all across the world. Share photos, watch videos, blog, order photo prints, or read some reviews by community members.

Site	Google	Alexa	Compete
http://www.helpfulvideo.com	4	309,044	540,231

Helpfulvideo.com is a website to share videos about everyday knowledge and skills with everyday people.

http://www.zeec.net	4	559,936	0

A nice, simple site to share your photos and videos.

http://www.panjea.com	4	687,155	749,824

This site enables you to pull video from YouTube, Yahoo, MySpaceTV, and Google to mix it with other clips. You can then post the end product on your own site or back to a video sharing site.

http://www.hungryflix.com	4	760,716	1,280,972

HungryFlix provides downloads for your iPod, iPhone, PSP, Apple TV, or your computer.

http://www.qubetv.tv	4	1,103,919	713,273

QubeTV.tv is dedicated to bringing your conservative take on politics and culture to the Internet.

http://www.vidipedia.org	4	1,230,848	0

The free video encyclopedia that anyone can edit.

http://uvu.channel2.org	4	1,371,073	261,244

Watch a program, performance, or lecture and instantly share your view with the rest of the South Florida community.

Site	Google	Alexa	Compete
http://www.yurth.com	4	2,585,858	0

Combined with Google Earth, this site allows you to find video based on where in the world it came from.

http://www.caught-on-video.com	3	131,796	99,353
http://www.funmansion.com	3	171,280	118,384
http://www.funnyreign.com	3	241,682	108,194
http://www.mediabum.com	3	306,192	163,789
http://www.zanyvideos.com	3	714,247	234,295

Watch for this site to rise in the rankings.

http://www.danerd.com	3	736,268	618,399
http://www.cozmo.tv	3	958,386	280,219

Site re-named to www.coull.com

http://www.skilltip.tv	3	1,142,039	1,889,616

11. Coordinate Your Social Media

Friends, followers and Customer Evangelists started with 450 sites.

Even after weeding out sites that no longer exist and the marketing sites, there are still more than 300 sites remaining. That's a lot to keep up with. Anyone who has an account with Facebook, LinkedIn, and Twitter will tell you that just keeping up with those three takes a significant amount of time and energy.

Fortunately, there are a few simple ways to make using social media easier and coordinate your efforts:
1. start with your username and password
2. plan your social media time (doing it and learning it)
3. use services to actively coordinate your activity

Start with Your Username and Password

Ever since the internet started, and especially since companies were developed to protect your identity, we've been told to use a separate username and password for every account.

In all fairness, I don't think anyone was anticipating having hundreds of social media sites, multiple e-mail accounts, online banking, and millions of membership sites. Trying to keep track of all those usernames and passwords would be a full-time job.

Whether you're new to social media, new to the internet, or an old-hand at surfing the dataflow, my suggestion is that you start with OpenID.

OpenID, in their own words is *"an open, decentralized, free framework for user-centric digital identity."*

In everyday language, it means you can use one username and password to access a whole lot of different sites. That's very useful.

The sites you use an OpenID for are social media, e-mail, and blogs. For the most part, none of these sites should have any truly personal information on them (phone numbers, social security numbers, or credit card numbers), so security isn't an issue. Besides, when a company like VeriSign is a provider for OpenID (and it is) you know it's safe to use.

In fact, there are five main providers for OpenID.

- ✓ http://claimID.com
- ✓ http://myid.net
- ✓ http://www.myopenid.com
- ✓ http://myvidoop.com
- ✓ http://pip.verisignlabs.com

Simply go to any of these sites to register and obtain your OpenID.

Of course, the big question is: Where can you use an OpenID?

The short answer is that there are literally hundreds of sites that allow you to use OpenID for your username and password. You can get a complete list of the sites that use OpenID at https://www.myopenid. com/directory.

Some of the larger sites allow you to use your existing information as an OpenID. They have specific instructions for each site. Here are instructions from OpenID.net to help you out:

> *If you use any of the following services, you already have your own OpenID. (When you see **bold** text, you should replace it with your own username, screenname or membername on the service.)*
>
> AOL
> openid.aol.com/**screenname**
>
> Google
> Look for the "Sign in with a Google Account" button
>
> MySpace
> Look for the "Login with MySpaceID" button or enter myspace.com/**username**
>
> Yahoo!
> Look for the "Sign in with Yahoo! ID" button
>
> Blogger
> **blogname**.blogspot.com
>
> Flickr
> Look for the "Sign in with Yahoo! ID" button or enter www.flickr.com/photos/username

LiveDoor
profile.livedoor.com/**username**

LiveJournal
username.livejournal.com

SmugMug
username.smugmug.com

Technorati
technorati.com/people/technorati/**username**

Vox
member.vox.com

WordPress.com
username.wordpress.com

You can see that OpenID is a widely accepted platform for accessing a lot of reputable, reliable sites. The only suggestion I have for using OpenID is that you treat your password with respect. Design it as a high-security password and make sure it stays private.

A good way to design a high-security password is with a cookbook or dictionary. (If you're using a cookbook, I recommend The Joy of Cooking because it has several hundred pages.) Here's how to do it:

1. Plan to use a password of 8 to 12 characters
2. Flip the cookbook or dictionary open to a random page
3. Close your eyes and place your finger on one of the pages
4. The character your finger covers is the first character of your password (avoid using fractions if that's what your finger hits)
5. Repeat this process until you have 8 to 12 characters
6. Flip the book open to a random page and choose one of the characters from the page number (Do this step at least twice)
7. Use the numbers from step 6 to locate characters in your password and make those characters uppercase letters
8. You now have a high-security password

One of the reasons this works well with a cookbook is they always contain numbers in the recipes. It's always a good idea to mix numbers in with letters to make your password. If it happens that you don't get any numbers while you're picking characters, you should replace at least two characters with a randomly selected number.

Since there are some sites that don't use OpenID, you're probably still going to need to choose a username and password.

My suggestion is that you try to use the same username as often as possible, and always use the same password. On occasion, you may find the username you want to use has been taken. Just put "the" in front of your username, and that generally solves the problem. To be sure you'll always be able to use the same username, use an e-mail address – they're always unique.

Once you've decided how to register for your social media sites – OpenID or individual usernames and passwords for each site – you need to think about how much time you're going to put into social media.

Plan Your Social Media Time (Doing It and Learning It)

Start with planning 30 minutes each day to learn about social media. This is when you will visit one site – just one – and learn about that site. Sign up for an account, complete your profile, and look at what the site offers. (Keep in mind that you can always close an account if you decide you don't want to use a site.)

Being a member really is the only way to honestly evaluate how useful a site is for you.

Be sure to visit the FAQ pages of any site you join. These pages have useful information and reading them can keep you from making the mistake of asking an FAQ in one of the forums or in a group. You'll find people are quick to point out when you should be reading the FAQ pages if you make that particular mistake.

When you're finished reading the FAQ pages for a site, it's time to switch from learning to doing. You'll still be learning as you go along, but now you can take that 30 minutes of learning time each day and use it to find other sites to explore.

When it comes to *doing* on a social media site, I like to use the menu from the site as a guide. Here's my home page from LinkedIn as an example.

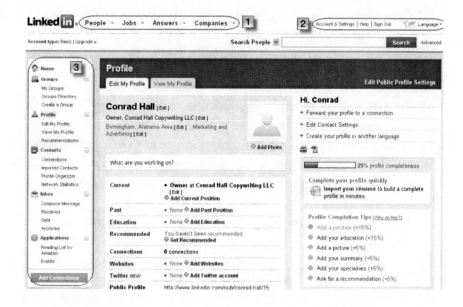

On LinkedIn, there are three areas you can work with to learn about using the site:

1. Quick Select Menu
2. Help Menu
3. Personal Menu

These menus are common to most sites. They look a little different from site to site, and some sites will have more menus than just these, but these three are fundamental to every successful site.

To access any of these menus, you do have to be signed in to the site.

1. Quick Select Menu

This is where you can move to general features of the site.

In the case of LinkedIn, the quick select menu allows you to search for people and companies, browse through jobs, ask questions, read answers, or find questions to answer.

On any site, you're going to meet people when you use this menu. You'll see what they're talking about and how they interact. This is a vital part of getting to know how you should behave within the site.

Using this menu can also give you some ideas for using your personal menu. When you find a person, see what groups they belong to – then you can use your personal menu to join that group.

When you find someone sharing something you're interested in, use your personal menu to add them to your contacts.

2. Help Menu

The help menu is where, in addition to general help topics, you often find the FAQ, support, and contact information, etc. It's also where you can change your account settings and logout from the site.

The account settings are a good place to spend time learning about the site. This is where you set options for how often the site sends you updates, whether your profile is public or private, and who is allowed to contact you through the site.

We've already spoken about FAQ pages. Be sure to read through these because there are all kinds of useful tidbits that will definitely help you get the most from your social media experience.

Other things you'll find in the help menu are support pages (how to contact support or submit a support ticket), learning center pages (i.e. learn about how to use the site and get the most from it), and the site's Privacy Policy and Terms of Use.

Now, I know reading a Terms of Use page is about as much fun as watching grass grow. That doesn't keep it from being in your best interest to read one or two of these. Seriously. They're all fairly similar, so you really do need to read only one or two – and you should do it.

Aside from getting a better understanding of your privileges and responsibilities (you really don't have too many "rights" when it comes to social media), reading one of these actually helped me understand the whole system better. That's why I'm recommending you read at least one Terms of Use page.

3. Personal Menu

We covered a little bit of the personal menu to show how it ties into the quick select menu. But there's a whole lot more to it than that.

The personal menu is the most important part of any social media site.

This is where you fill in your profile, post updates, join groups, add contacts, answer messages, and use applications. As you can imagine, completing your profile is the single most important thing you can do on any social media site.

Your profile is how people find out who you are. From your name to your hobbies and business pursuits, the profile is the foundation of your presence in social media. To make the best use of it, copy the information from your profile into a Word document, spell check it, and save it. Then you can use it again and again to complete your profile on other sites.

By the time you complete your profile on each of these sites, you will have spent a significant amount of time thinking about what you want to say to the people you're going to meet. Compiling the information from the profiles on these three sites will make filling in a profile on any other site a breeze.

Once your profile is complete, you'll want to add some contacts. Start with your e-mail address book – from a service like Gmail or Yahoo, or from Outlook. After all, you're joining a site to be social, right? Who better to be social with than people you already know.

It's even better if they turn out to already be a member of the site. Not only can you socialize, you can pick their brains about how to use the site.

Posting updates is how you stay involved in the community of the site, but even more fun – and important – is the groups feature.

Joining a site like Facebook or even LinkedIn (which is well targeted to business) is akin to walking into a conference hall that's hosting every conference in existence at the same time. It can be just a little noisy and confusing.

Finding a group means you're finding people who have a mutual interest in something. You get to cut the noise down to conversations you can join and follow. Just be careful about how many groups you join.

You should be careful about the topics you pursue by joining groups. Check out Jim Turner's profile on LinkedIn and you'll see he belongs to 31 LinkedIn groups – and they're all related to his business. That's the important part.

When you're using social media to grow your business, stay focused on business when you're choosing groups to join. Does that mean a person who sells shoes shouldn't join an amateur photography group even though she really enjoys taking pictures? No, it doesn't mean that.

What it means is that you have to pay attention to how much time you're putting into social media. Jim puts hours into it every day because it is his principle means for acquiring new clients. A salesperson might want to limit her time in social media to an hour or an hour and half each day. That means having to carefully choose the groups with which she will and will not interact.

By all means, participate in activities that you enjoy. You'll find the personal menu on a site often includes the opportunity to post photos, videos, book lists, and other ways of expressing your individuality. One key to being successful with social media, and making the most of your time, is to use just one site for pursuing those interests.

Focusing on one site allows you to use your profile link from that site to show people where they can learn more about you. Drive traffic to that one site (okay, two sites when you count LinkedIn and Facebook – Twitter doesn't have these bells and whistles) and spend your time building an identity there.

You might join and participate in several social media sites, but that doesn't mean you have to duplicate every last item from one site to the next.

And for the things you will duplicate across several sites – status updates in particular – there are some tools that make your life much, much easier.

Use Services to Effectively Coordinate Your Activity

Even when you're a member of just the Golden Trio posting the same status update to all three is a tedious, time-consuming task.

That's where an updating service comes in (a.k.a. social media aggregator). Any one of these services allows you to post status updates across several sites at once, and two of them allow you to post across dozens in one fell swoop. Two others allow you to see status updates from your friends as well as make posts.

This is where it gets interesting – where you balance streamlining your efforts with making social media personal.

Remember that the personal menu allows you to do much more than just write a status update. That's really just one thing you can do on the home page of any social media site. The personal menu also opens you up to finding groups, new contacts, uploading and watching video, and posting photos.

You can see how using a service to coordinate your posting activity really is just cutting down the time it takes to keep friends and followers informed. We still have to visit individual sites to truly participate in a community. It's only by visiting a site that you can participate in groups and post media (photos and video).

With that in mind, let's take a look at some of the services that make coordinating your social media easier. (The list is in alphabetical order.)

Flock

Site	Google	Alexa	Compete
www.flock.com	8	15,516	17,737

Flock is a browser – just like Firefox or Internet Explorer.

The difference between other browsers and Flock is that Flock is designed to enable you to stay logged-in to your social media accounts. Currently, Flock supports 18 social media sites – networking, bookmarking, and video. (This is the only aggregator that connects to YouTube.)

The way it works is that you connect Flock to your Twitter, Facebook, YouTube, or other social media accounts. Then you tell Flock to remember each account as you connect it to the browser. Each time you open Flock, it automatically logs you in to each site (just as Firefox allows you to save tabs when you close it).

FriendFeed

Site	Google	Alexa	Compete
www.friendfeed.com	8	897	1880

FriendFeed approaches the idea of coordinating your social media by making you the center of attention.

Rather than you sending updates out to multiple services, it pulls anything you do on those services into your FriendFeed account. When you publish a photo on Flickr –an update is generated in your FriendFeed account. You can even connect it to your blog so people get updated when you make a blog post, too.

What you do is invite your friends to connect with you on FriendFeed. Then they can subscribe to your feed and you can subscribe to theirs. While you're on the site, you receive updates in real time – no need to refresh your browser.

Hellotxt

Site	Google	Alexa	Compete
www.hellotxt.com	7	27,588	51,008

Hellotext.com connects you to 58 social media sites – networking, bookmarking, and video.

You can update your account in several ways:
- ✓ e-mail
- ✓ SMS (Short Message Service for your mobile device)
- ✓ Google Talk
- ✓ MSN
- ✓ Yahoo

For example, when you send an update to Hellotxt.com by e-mail, you can include a media attachment. Any photo or video you send with the e-mail will be hosted by Hellotxt.com.

Just be careful with the e-mail address – or any address – you get for sending updates. There is no barrier to posting an update. If you give an address to someone, they can post to your account.

Hellotxt.com also allows you to ad your Google Adsense code to your account. They will display your ads half the time and their ads half the time. It's a neat way to make some extra cash while you're networking. (Although I'm not sure how much anyone will appreciate having ads with your posts.)

Minggl

Site	Google	Alexa	Compete
www.minggl.com	5	271,146	802,377

This is a downloadable toolbar that I've been using for a little while.

It currently connects to six sites (MySpace, LinkedIn, Flickr, Facebook, twitter, Digg) and gives you access to all the personal menu items you find on each site. Each site is listed in the toolbar with a drop down menu. The drop down menu is what gives you access to the features associated with each site.

OnlyWire

Site	Google	Alexa	Compete
www.onlywire.com	5	6,620	14,398

This is primarily a bookmarking site that updates 30 social media sites with content every time you bookmark a page.

It is also the only site I've looked at that I would consider using the paid option – primarily because it's only $24.99 per year. The main difference between the free and paid service is that the free service is supported by ads. Two dollars a month is a reasonable price to pay for being ad-free.

The free version also requires you to add the OnlyWire button to your website. If you don't add the button, they will close your account. It actually works out in your favor to have the button since it increases traffic by giving visitors another option for sharing what they like.

A nice feature in OnlyWire is that it shows every site to which an update has been made. This is handy when one of the sites doesn't update for any reason. OnlyWire highlights it by putting "failure" in bright red letters. (That has helped me find misspelled passwords twice.)

Ping

Site	Google	Alexa	Compete
www.ping.fm	5	51,405	23,281

Ping gives you access to 38 social media sites – networking, bookmarking, and video.

It has a toolbar that let's you jump to the sign-in page, access popular blogs, and send updates (once you're signed in).

Ping is great for updating multiple services at once – just like Hellotxt.com. What neither of these services can do is give you the two-way communication you get with Minggl. The advantage Ping.fm and Hellotxt.com have is that they connect to a large number of sites from one place.

Spread The Funkyness

Site	Google	Alexa	Compete
http://spreadingfunkyness.com/posty	3	1,031,424	1,125,836

Posty is similar to Ping and Hellotxt.com, but it only connects to five social media sites: Twitter, Jaiku, Tumblr, FriendFeed, and Identi.ca.

It's interesting that Posty connects to FriendFeed (the other services don't) because FriendFeed is a social media aggregator, too.

Sendible

Site	Google	Alexa	Compete
www.sendible.com	4	321,947	3,166,109

This is the only one of the services listed that is a paid service. It has five membership levels.

	Basic Free forever!	Pro Cancel anytime!	Small Business Cancel anytime!	Enterprise Cancel anytime!	Online Marketer Cancel anytime!
Price per month	Free/month	$ 3.00/month	$ 9.00/month	$ 35.00/month	$ 6.00/month
Messages and Status Updates	100/month	350/month	2000/month	15000/month	1000/month
Contacts	300	750	1500	10000	2000
File attachments per message	1	1	5	20	1
Number of contact groups	1	5	20	100	10
Free SMS Credits per month *	None	25	100	250	None
Messages are free of advertising	✗	✓	✓	✓	✓
Widgets	✗	✓	✓	✓	✓
Email, SMS and Social Messaging	✓	✓	✓	✓	✓
Status updates contain "via Sendible"	✓	✗	✗	✗	✗
	Sign Up!	Sign Up!	Sign Up!	Sign Up!	Sign Up!

I have a free account with Sendible to be able to do research, but it seems a bit much to pay for a service that puts limits on my activity when I can get the same service for free – without limits.

Sendible only has eight social media sites –five for networking and three for blogging. It does also give you access to six different e-mail providers. That's unique – the other services don't bother with e-mail.

Steamy

Site	Google	Alexa	Compete
www.streamy.com	6	86,471	145,722

Streamy is similar to Flock.

It's similar to Flock because it allows you to be logged in to several sites at the same time. The interface is a little nicer with Streamy. Instead of having tabs in a browser, Streamy has icons across the top of the screen. When you want to access your Twitter account, just click on the Twitter icon.

Right now, Streamy has only nine services and four of them are AOL, Google Talk, Yahoo and Live. This service will definitely be better as they add more services.

Summary

You can see how some of these services can be used in combination. For example, I use Ping to send status updates to multiple sites, FriendFeed to keep everything in one spot for people who want to pay attention to me, and Minggl to interact with my groups and other features on the larger sites.

Streamy is a service I'm starting to use, and I think you can watch for a battle to play out between Minggl and Streamy. They're quite similar services with the dividing line being between people who like using toolbars (Minggl) and others who prefer to use a browser window (Streamy).

My suggestion is that you start with FriendFeed. This makes it easy for your friends, and you, to stay up-to-date. Everything is in one spot so all you have to take care of is connecting a new account to your FriendFeed account. When you're familiar with FriendFeed, you can venture on to work with the other services listed here.

And what about the social media sites that aren't connected to these services? After all, there are over 300 social media sites listed in this guide and the most any one service connects to is 58.

My answer is to go back to Jim Turner's advice. Start with the Golden Trio – Facebook, Twitter, and LinkedIn. All the services, except one, connect to these three social media sites.

Then look at which other social media sites are connected to these services. You know they're in the business of giving people what they want, so each service is going to focus on connecting to the popular social media sites. Pick out the ones that suit you and join them.

For the sites left over – the ones that don't have large audiences – updating them manually might be the effort you put out to connect with a niche market.

Index of Sites

Appendix A – New Sites

These are sites that are literally new this year or that were overlooked. Yes, it's true, I missed sites that I'm actually a member of. Imagine that!

My blog, www.TheMarketingSpotlight.com is a Wordpress blog, but I completely missed adding Wordpress.com this year. I apologize to the folks at Wordpress, and to each of the other sites that I missed.

All of these sites will be integrated into the main listings when the guide is updated for 2011. In addition, we'll be adding a section just for blogging.

There are so many sites for building your own blog that it can support being its own section. Judging from how many new ones have come out this year, I think you'll also see a much larger section for social media aggregators.

Site	Google	Alexa	Compete
http://www.google.com/talk/	10	1	1

This is an instant messaging service. It does have an option that allows you to video chat.

http://www.facebook.com/pages	9	4	3

This is an extension of Facebook. For businesses, this is a great way to develop a dialogue with your customers.

http://wordpress.com/	9	19	36

When you get a blog on this site, Wordpress is hosting your blog. That means they control it.

Site	Google	Alexa	Compete
http://wordpress.org	9	508	1256

When you get a Wordpress blog from this site, you need your own hosting account. This means you host your own blog, and you control it.

Both Wordpress sites are free to use. For businesses, the best option is definitely Wordpress.org. It gives you complete freedom to do what you want with your blog.

There are thousands of Wordpress plugins that let you connect your blog to other social media. Visit www.michelfortin.com (his blog) and do a search for "plugins." Michel has posted some terrific articles that show every plugin he uses and what they do.

http://www.flickr.com/	9	31	33

This is a photo and video sharing site. It has good tools for handling your photos and video.

https://www.blogger.com	8	8	25

You can guess from the name – this is a site where you get to create your own blog.

http://www.typepad.com	8	215	119

This is a blogging site. You create you own blog and can connect it to other social media sites.

https://friendfeed.com/	8	891	1880

FriendFeed is the best social media aggregator I've seen.

FriendFeed pulls your content in from other sites. You name the sites you belong to, give FriendFeed access and then FriendFeed keeps your profile updated with information from those sites. Anyone who subscribes to your FriendFeed gets a personal notification in whichever format they choose.

Site	Google	Alexa	Compete
http://www.vox.com/	8	1214	1455

This is a blogging site.

http://photobucket.com/	7	41	40

This is a photo and video sharing site.

http://www.tuenti.com/	7	242	107182

Social networking in Spanish.

http://www.imeem.com/	7	247	113

A music sharing site.

http://tumblr.com/	7	544	637

A blogging site.

https://www.plaxo.com/	7	1465	681

A social networking site.

http://www.plurk.com/	7	1580	7864

A "social journal" for your life.

http://posterous.com/	7	3381	N/A

This site works almost like a storage space. You don't sign up for an account – you just send them an e-mail and they reply with a link to whatever you sent.

You can post video, mp3, files – anything you like.

Site	Google	Alexa	Compete
https://www.rememberthemilk.com/	7	7650	10933

Your online "To Do" list. Just what we need…one more way to stay disorganized.

http://identi.ca/	7	10723	23296

A Twitter clone.

http://brightkite.com/	7	11375	7604

A cross between Facebook and Twitter. You can login to this site using your Facebook information.

http://laconi.ca	7	32946	95401

This site is in Private BETA and has changed its name to http://status.net.

You can sign up to be notified when the site goes into public use mode.

http://www.skyrock.com/	6	57	12388

A multi-lingual social networking site.

http://www.tagged.com/	6	85	128

A social networking site with – they claim – 80 million members.

http://blip.fm/	6	3948	4722

Your replacement for Pandora. Blip connects with several social media sites, and has no limits on how much music you can listen to each month.

Watch for this site to rise in the rankings.

Site	Google	Alexa	Compete
http://seesmic.com/	6	14577	10580

This is an application you can use in your browser, on your desktop or with your phone. It is an aggregator for Facebook and Twitter. They have a way to go before they can compete with FriendFeed.

http://www.socialmedian.com/	6	23177	27390

This is a site where you can get the news – only it's filtered by your contacts.

http://jiwai.de	6	23595	746444

This is a social networking site in, I think, Japanese.

http://12seconds.tv/	6	29409	11223

Think Twitter on video. You upload short videos instead of a 140 character statement. It also connects to several other social media sites.
Watch for this site to rise in the rankings.

https://www.yammer.com/	6	44039	21288

This is a social network for businesses. You have to use a valid business e-mail, and you will only be able to connect with other people at your workplace.

http://www.utterli.com/	6	46319	67059

A Twitter-like site that gives you no information until after you sign up.

http://youare.com/	6	60206	113154

A Twitter clone.

Site	Google	Alexa	Compete
http://my.mashable.com/	5	823	828

Watch for this blog to skyrocket in the rankings!

Mashable is currently #3 on the Technorati Top 100 – last week it was #9.

This blog is about all things social media and technology. I've had an opportunity to exchange a couple of e-mails with Pete Cashmore (Mashable's founder), and he seems like a nice fellow focused on delivering useful content. I like this site.

http://digu.com/	5	23126	561297

Social networking in, I think, Chinese.

SPECIAL NOTE: I'm tucking this away in here for people who really are reading. Watch for social media sites to be developed in Chinese. It's an emerging market, and seeing social media sites in either Mandarin or Cantonese will be a huge sign that China is opening up to the world.

http://zuosa.com/	5	24652	706026

A Twitter look-alike, only in – I think – Japanese.

http://www.kwippy.com/	5	70614	163705

A Twitter clone.

http://radar.net/	5	76963	74467

Social Media for your cell phone.

This service integrates with Twitter, Facebook, Flickr and other social media sites. Watch for this site to rise in the rankings.

http://www.koornk.com/	5	84213	151667

A Twitter clone.

Site	Google	Alexa	Compete
http://www.feecle.jp/	5	129271	1274828

I'm not sure. I think the site is written in Korean.

http://buboo.tw/	5	142882	2341358

Social networking in Korean (I think).

https://presentlyapp.com/	5	221093	143605

This is a Twitter clone designed specifically for business to use privately. You can set up your own internal network to let employees collaborate.

http://www.shoutem.com/	4	42244	191511

This is a Twitter clone you can use with your own membership site. You can set up your own micro-blogging community and keep it private.

http://www.meemi.com/	4	117139	658560

Their tagline is "all noise around you." It's a twitter clone.

http://jisko.net/	4	183636	749919

This site is in BETA.
It is a Spanish version of Twitter.

http://usa.streetmavens.com/	4	223961	285883

This site is in BETA.
This is a Twitter clone designed to focus on local events. You can find out what is happening in your town, or around the globe.

Site	Google	Alexa	Compete
http://mexicodiario.com/	4	481548	3270948

A Twitter clone for Mexico.

http://buzzherd.com/	4	593454	2051859

This site is designed specifically for business owners. It is different from LinkedIn because this site lets you build a website and establish a blog in addition to making referrals and networking.

http://plerb.com/	3	420556	891913

This is a Twitter clone.

http://numpa.com/	0	1462615	3271258

Twitter for the Netherlands.

Appendix B – Removed Sites

In this appendix, the sites are listed alphabetically with a capital letter beside each site name. The capital letter indicates whether the site is for
- ✓ Bookmarking
- ✓ Networking, or
- ✓ Video

Most of these sites have been removed simply because they no longer exist, but that isn't the only reason for a site to be removed from the guide. Some of these sites have been removed because they are a business site rather than a social media site.

http://ma.gnolia.com	B
http://mix.lycos.com	V
http://mojiti.com	V
http://my.xilinus.com	B
http://myweb.yahoo.com	B
http://soapbox.msn.com	V
http://stage6.divx.com	V
http://start.aimpages.com	N
http://strmz.jot.com	V
http://supr.c.ilio.us	B
http://uncutV.aol.com	V
http://V-upload.download.com	V
http://www.100millionspiders.com	N
http://www.2centsnews.com	B
http://www.30daytags.com	B
http://www.6-clicks.com	B
http://www.9rules.com	B
http://www.addictingclips.com	V
http://www.akintu.com	N

http://www.allyourwords.com	B
http://www.babbello.com	N
http://www.bigcontact.com	V
http://www.bizfriendz.com	N
http://www.bizpreneur.com	N
http://www.blinkbits.com	B
http://www.blinklist.com	B
http://www.bluedot.us	N
http://www.bmaccess.net	B
http://www.bofunk.com	V
http://www.broadcaster.com	N
http://www.broadcaster.com	V
http://www.bumpzee.com	B
http://www.canyouconnect.com	N
http://www.castpost.com	V
http://www.christianspace360.com	N
http://www.clickcaster.com	V
http://www.clipfire.com	B
http://www.communityx.net	N
http://www.cuts.com	V
http://www.dave.tv	V
http://www.daylo.com	N
http://www.dodgeball.com	N
http://www.dohat.com	B
http://www.dotcomedy.com	V
http://www.dovetail.tv	V
http://www.dumpthe.net	V
http://www.eVshare.com	V
http://www.eyespot.com	V
http://www.fark.com/V/	V
http://www.fazed.org	B
http://www.feedmelinks.com	B
http://www.filecow.com	V
http://www.fireant.tv	V

http://www.fliqz.com	V
http://www.flurl.com	V
http://www.fungow.com	B
http://www.funnydump.com	V
http://www.furl.com	B
http://www.furl.net	B
http://www.gibeo.net	B
http://www.glumbert.com	V
http://www.godtube.com	V
http://www.greatestjournal.com	N
http://www.grouper.com	V
http://www.hanzoweb.com	B
http://www.hyperlinkomatic.com	B
http://www.ifilm.com	V
http://www.intellectconnect.com	N
http://www.itsjustcoffee.com	N
http://www.izimi.com	V
http://www.jumpcut.com	V
http://www.kinja.com	B
http://www.kwego.com	V
http://www.lifelogger.com	B
http://www.lifelogger.com	V
http://www.lilisto.com	B
http://www.linknrank.com	N
http://www.listible.com	B
http://www.listmixer.com	B
http://www.lunarstorm.co.uk	N
http://www.maniatv.com	V
http://www.markaboo.com	B
http://www.meme-stream.com	B
http://www.memfrag.com	B
http://www.mixednutz.net	N
http://www.mixpo.com	V
http://www.mogulus.com	V

http://www.mugshot.org	N
http://www.myextreme.ca	V
http://www.mynetspot.org	N
http://www.myvmarks.com	B
http://www.needforfun.com	V
http://www.nelsok.com	V
http://www.newsweight.com	B
http://www.onfuego.com	V
http://www.openserving.com	B
http://www.operator11.com	V
http://www.philoi.com	B
http://www.pickle.com	V
http://www.pixelmo.com	B
http://www.pixparty.com	V
http://www.plugim.com	B
http://www.plum.com	B
http://www.portachi.com	B
http://www.pureV.com	V
http://www.putfile.com	V
http://www.ruckus.com	N
http://www.shadows.com	B
http://www.sharkle.com	V
http://www.shoppersbase.com	B
http://www.shoutfile.com	V
http://www.shoutwire.com	B
http://www.sitespaces.net	N
http://www.sitetagger.com	B
http://www.smelis.com	B
http://www.spotplex.com	B
http://www.spurl.net	B
http://www.student.com	N
http://www.stupidVs.com	V
http://www.syncone.net	B
http://www.taggly.com	B

http://www.tailrank.com	B
http://www.tektag.com	B
http://www.thatVsite.com	V
http://www.thoof.com	B
http://www.truveo.com	V
http://www.tubearoo.com	V
http://www.u2upfly.com	V
http://www.udugu.com	N
http://www.unalog.com	B
http://www.urlex.info	B
http://www.uuswap.com	N
http://www.V123.com	V
http://www.Vbomb.com	V
http://www.Vdumper.com	V
http://www.Vwebtown.com	V
http://www.vidilife.com	V
http://www.vlogmap.org	V
http://www.vmix.com	V
http://www.voomed.com	V
http://www.vshake.com	N
http://www.vsocial.com	V
http://www.vume.com	V
http://www.vuze.com	V
http://www.web-feeds.com	B
http://www.wewin.com	V
http://www.wink.com	B
http://www.wirefan.com	B
http://www.youare.tv	V
http://www.yourkindatv.com	V
http://www.ziddio.com	V
http://www.zippyVs.com	V
http://www.zlitt.com	B

Appendix C – Video Resources

Since video looks harder than it is, I decided to include an appendix with resources that make getting started with video easier. Most of these resources are free.

And let me offer a bit of advice from my own experience: Sometimes the easiest thing to do is just sit down and record something as a video. For me it didn't matter what it was, I just recorded myself talking about being scared of making a video and making some silly noises.

After that, it got a lot easier to "be serious" about putting videos together.

Techniques and Equipment

How to Make Your YouTube Videos Look Great
http://www.squidoo.com/youtuberight (by Juan M. Parra, a.k.a. Cinetech)

This is a Squidoo lens dedicated to helping everyone make their videos look as good as possible on YouTube. There is also a link to another lens Juan has made that goes into tremendous detail about how to shoot video specifically for use on the web.

I suggest bookmarking both pages rather than printing the information. They take up quite a few pages if you print them, and since both web pages are Squidoo lenses you can be sure Juan will be updating them as new information becomes available.

How to Shoot, Edit, Promote, and Publish Your Video
http://makeInternettv.org

I mentioned this site earlier in Chapter 9 – What is Video Sharing.

This site is exhaustive in its coverage of all things related to video. My suggestion is that you start with Juan's lenses and build on that knowledge by going to internettv.org. You'll be able to return to this site over and over to find answers to your questions.

Buying Guide for Video Cameras
http://google-cnet.com.com/camcorder-buying-guide

CNET is one of the top sites for up-to-date, accurate and easy-to-understand information on all things technical. They have a large number of newsletters (because of the numerous topics they cover), and I recommend making time to review what they offer. I don't know anyone who has gone to www.cnet.com and subscribed to any less than two of their newsletters.

Video Camera Shopping Guide
http://www.camcorderinfo.com

I decided to list this equipment guide because Juan cited it in his Squidoo lens on how to shoot video for the web.

This site has ratings and reviews for every video camera in existence (I think). It even has a free video library with stock footage of hard to reach locations you can use.

Video Converters
In Chapter 9 – What is Video Sharing, I mentioned 6 different formats for video. Something I didn't mention – because I knew it goes here – is that you can increase how often your videos are watched by uploading them in the different formats to different video sites.

Just as some people like Internet Explore and others swear by Firefox, lots of people have preferences for video file format. So, to make your life easier, here is a list of sites where you can put your videos into different formats.

Each of these sites has you upload your video to their site, they make the conversion, then send you an e-mail with a link so you can download the converted file. Only Hey Watch! is a paid service, but even that is surprisingly inexpensive. You can convert 6 – 1hr videos into three different formats each month for less than 5 dollars.

Zamzar (www.zamzar.com)
This site offers two level of use – both free. You can be a "guest" or a registered user. I suggest being a registered user because it lets you store files (up to 100GB), and your files get converted before "guests."

MediaConvert (http://media-convert.com)

This site offers you the choice between letting them do the conversion and downloading free software to do the conversions yourself. Either way, getting your files converted is free.

As a bonus, they have an audio file converter you can download for free, too.

Hey Watch! (http://heywatch.com)

This is the paid service, and it is quite inexpensive. They use a "credit" system where one credit allows you to have a 45 minute video converted. One credit costs $0.10 – ten cents. They even have a calculator at the bottom of their home page so you can get a cost estimate before signing up.

MediaConverter (www.mediaconverter.org)

I enjoy the clean, easy-to-use page on this site. It even has a "Mac-like" quality with the icons across the bottom of the screen. That's cool.

For the rest of these headings, I've decided to give you a list of the relevant sites and let you explore them. As with the social media sites, they all have just slightly different offerings so trying to describe each one would be just a little boring for the reader.

Would you like to make next year's guide even better? You can help by sending me an e-mail to say what you'd like to see included for this section next year. Just e-mail me at feedback@theconradhall. com. Every suggestion I use gets you a credit in the next edition of the *friends, followers and Customer Evangelists.*

Editing Sites

How well your video is edited plays a big part in getting that video to go viral. It's sort of like telling a joke – you can have the world's funniest joke, but nobody laughs when it's told poorly.

The sites are listed in alphabetical order.

- ✓ BubblePly (www.bubbleply.com)
- ✓ Cuts (www.cuts.com) – takes you to www.rifftrax.com/cuts
- ✓ Eyespot (www.eyespot.com) – takes you to PixelFish
- ✓ MixerCast (www.mixercast.com)
- ✓ Motionbox (www.motionbox.com)
- ✓ MovieMasher (www.moviemasher.com)
- ✓ Photobucket (www.photobucket.com)

✓ StashSpace (www.stashspace.com)

✓ Veotag (www.veotag.com)

✓ Vidavee Grafitti (http://graffiti.vidavee.com)

✓ Vmix (www.vmix.com) – a paid service

Search Sites

These sites are similar to a vertical search engine. They only search videos, and they can help you find examples of videos you can mimic when you make your own.

The sites are listed in alphabetical order.

✓ Blinkx (www.blinkx.com)

✓ ClipRoller (www.cliproller.com)

✓ Google Video Search (http://video.google.com)

✓ Pixsy (www.pixsy.com)

✓ PureVideo (www.purevideo.com)

✓ ScoopVid (www.scoopvid.com)

✓ Search For Video (www.searchforvideo.com)

✓ Truveo (www.truveo.com)

✓ TubeSurf (www.tubesurf.com)

✓ Yahoo! Video Search (http://video.search.yahoo.com)

Downloading Services

These sites enable you to download videos you want to keep – mostly from YouTube, but some of them allow you to download from other sites, too.

Pay attention to the instructions on each site. Most of them require you to change the file extension to .flv after the download is complete. That's because the site is changing the format of the file to Flash, but for some reason doesn't change the file extension.

✓ Kcoolonline (www.kcoolonline.com)

✓ KeepVid (www.keepvid.com)

✓ KissYouTube (www.kissyoutube.com)

✓ VideoDL ((www.videodl.org)

✓ VideoDownloader (https://addons.mozilla.org/en-US/firefox/addon/2390)

✓ Vixy (www.vixy.net)

✓ YouTubeDownloads (http://youtubedownloader.us/youtubedownloaderus.php)

✓ YouTubia (www.youtubia.com)

Vidcasts and Vlogging Sites

Vlogging is Video Blogging, and a Vidcast is a Video Podcast (internet TV).

These sites either provide you with a place to host your video blog, or give you resources to embed video on your existing blog.

- ✓ Ask a Ninja (www.askaninja.com)
- ✓ Digg Videos (http://digg.com/videos)
- ✓ DL.TV (http://dl.tv/)
- ✓ Revision3 (www.revision3.com)
- ✓ This Week in Tech (www.twit.tv)

Mobile Applications

The cell phone is the point of convergence for technology.

Until a new device is invented that allows us to wear our cell phones, put a screen over at least one eye, and operate it with voice commands, the cell phone is the convergence point for communications technology today. These sites will help you adapt your videos for display on cell phones equipped with video playback (or just watch some mind-numbing TV on your phone).

- ✓ Shozu (www.shozu.com/portal/index.do)
- ✓ Yahoo Mobile (http://mobile.yahoo.com/)
- ✓ MobiTV (www.mobitv.com/index2.php)
- ✓ MTV Mobile Video (www.mtv.com/mobile/video)
- ✓ Moblr (www.moblr.com/web.html)
- ✓ Mobunga (www.mobunga.com)

Other Tools

- ✓ Hellodeo (www.hellodeo.com)
- ✓ Flixn (www.flixn.com) – Paid service
- ✓ Bubble Guru (www.bubbleguru.com) – Paid service. This one is cool (a little limited in the number of videos you can use – max of 10, but cool)
- ✓ WebcamMax (www.webcammax.com) – Paid software
- ✓ StumbleUpon Video (http://video.stumbleupon.com)
- ✓ ClipSync (www.clipsync.com) – Paid service
- ✓ ClipSyndicate (www.clipsyndicate.com)

Appendix D – Your Profile Notes

There is lots of white space on each of these pages because you never know how much someone is going to want to write. It bugs me to no end when I get a book like this and there isn't enough white space for me to write what I want to put in.

Basic Information

Name: _____

Username: _____

_____

_____

Password: _____

Town: _____

Country: _____

Zip Code: _____

Relationship: _____

About You: _____

_____

_____

_____

There's lots of extra space here so you can write down more than one website URL, and so you can make note of the URLs for any other profiles you create on other sites.

This is also a good place to write down the contact information for Role Models you want to follow on the sites you join.

Contact Information

e-mail Address _____

website URL: _____

Telephone: _____

Fax: _____

Twitter URL: _____

Facebook URL: _____

LinkedIn URL: _____

Personal Information

Activities: _____

_____

_____

_____

Interests: _____

_____

_____

_____

Favorite Music: _____

_____

_____

Favorite TV: _____

_____

_____

Favorite Films: _____

_____

_____

Favorite Books: _____

_____

_____

Favorite Quotes: _____

_____

_____

Work Information

Current Position: _____

Company: _____

Description: _____
_____
_____

Current Position: _____

Company: _____

Description: _____
_____
_____

Past Position: _____

Company: _____

Description: _____
_____
_____

Past Position: _____

Company: _____

Description: _____
_____
_____

Education Information

High School: _____

Year Graduated: _____

College/University: _____

Major: _____

Year Graduated: _____

Additional Notes: _____
_____

Activities: _____
_____

College/University: _____

Major: _____

Year Graduated: _____

Additional Notes: _____
_____

Activities: _____
_____

Summary _____
_____
_____
_____

Specialties _____
_____
_____
_____

Sites I have Joined _____
_____
_____
_____
_____
_____
_____

Groups I have Joined _____
_____
_____
_____
_____
_____
_____

Appendix E – My Facebook Profile

This is how you get to your profile to edit it.

My Basic Information

Basic Information

Gender: **Male**

Hometown: **Toronto, ON**

Relationship Status: **Single**

Looking for: Networking

Political Views: Politics will make you sceptical

Religious views: Visit the widows and homeless in their distress.

My Activities & Interests

Personal Information

Activities: Photography, mostly nature and wildlife shots, but I'm getting better at shooting people; -)

Hiking, this is when I take the photos. I very much enjoy being outdoors and just looking for things to enjoy.

Camping, the tent and sleeping bag kind. Killarney Park in Ontario is simply wonderful for photos, hiking and camping.

Reading, Lots of reading, riding my bicycle - oh, and a little bit of writing every now and again.

Interests: People watching, it's better than the zoo.

One of my dreams is enough free time to learn how to play the piano and guitar.

Self-improvement, I have a definite interest in self-improvement. I suggest starting with "The Slight Edge" by Jeff Olson and building from there.

Notice how the name of the activity is separated from the description by a comma. The comma tells Facebook where a keyword ends.

Instead of writing "Photography," I could have written "Digital nature photography." That would have given Facebook a longer, more precise keyword phrase to use.

My reason for using more general keywords is that it allows people to start with a more general search. They can narrow it down to their particular interest after clicking on the keyword.

My Favorites

Favourite Music:	Classical, not a particular artist but the whole realm of classical music. It fascinates me that Bugs Bunny cartoons were set to classical music, and films like Platoon use it to stunning effect.
	I also enjoy blues, jazz, classic rock, and old country Red Sovine, Jim Reeves, Loretta Lynn
Favourite TV Programmes:	M.A.S.H., The longest running series in TV history, I think. They did a lot of firsts on M.A.S.H., and I watched it as a child, so it helped form some of my thought habits.
Favourite Films:	Where do I start? From John Wayne films to Christmas movies, from Bing Crosby and Fred Astaire to Liam Neeson and Matt Damon.
	Perhaps it's easiest to say my favourite kind of film is one with a message well told - even if that message is simply to make me laugh.
Favourite Books:	The Slight Edge, by Jeff Olson because it showed me the value of a penny, a drop of water, a single step.
	A Grief Observed, by C.S. Lewis because it healed my heart.
	Who Has Seen the Wind, by W.O. Mitchell because it taught me what a polymath is.
	Pilgrim's Progress, by John Bunyan because it challenged my spirit.
	Les Miserables, by Victor Hugo because it is a beautiful, tragic story.
Favourite Quotations:	**Life is a marathon. Be diligent. Finish Strong.** From Finish Strong by Dan Green.

You can increase the usefulness of your profile for other users by separating author and artist names with a comma, too. For example, with the books I've listed I could have written the entry for *The Slight Edge* like this:

The Slight Edge, Jeff Olson, Success Books, because it showed me...

This would allow other users to search Facebook for entries related to the title, author and publisher of the book.

For movies, TV programs and music, you can list artists, titles, writers or any other information you think other people might be interested in. As long as you separate each item with a comma, they'll be able to search Facebook for related entries.

Notice that the text for Favorite Quotations is not blue. That's because it's plain text. Facebook does not enable you to search for quotes on the site.

About Me

About me:

I live to write, to communicate, to teach.

My Aunt Geri was once upset with me because I pestered her for an answer. In her exasperation, she demanded "Do you have to have an answer for everything?"

I thought about that question long enough for Aunt Geri to forget about it. Then I answered "Yes."

"Yes, what?" she asked.

"Yes, I want to have an answer for everything."

Aunt Geri has since passed away. I honour her, and cherish her memory, by continuing to learn.

Contact Information

Contact Information

Email: conrad@conradhallcopywriting.com
                     spacekeeping@gmail.com

Current location: Toronto, ON

Website: http://www.TheMarketingSpotlight.com

My Groups

Groups   See All (5)

Member of: Bring Gary Vaynerchuk to Chicago. BROUGHT!!!, Affiliate Classroom
              2.0- Where the Super Affiliates was Born!, American Writers and
              Artists, Inc., Spread The Secret, Social Media Marketing Mastermind

Notice the text at the right side that says "See All (5)."

Clicking on that text opens a page where you see an icon and a description for each group. It works the same way for My Pages.

My Pages

Pages .... See All (8)

AWAI
Professional service

Social Media Marketing Best Practices
Technology product/service

Conrad Hall
Writer

SelfGrowth.com
Website

The Social Media Marketing Network
Professional service

My Facebook Profile URL

Memorable web address

Profile web address:	http://profile.to/conradhall/
Choose address:	Click here to choose or change your own memorable profile web address
Advanced Search:	Search Facebook for old friends, new friends or a date and display their profile web address

Appendix F – Blog Off Competition Details

Judging Criteria

1. Captivating blog headlines - how good are they?
2. Quality - what is the originality, depth and quality of writing?
3. Traffic - how many page visits were you able to generate for your content?
4. Dialog - how many people commented and how did you respond?
5. Length of visit - did your audience stay engaged?

The Reward

1st Place - $25,000* in International Prizes

✓ A feature interview with yourBusinessChannel.com. yBC reaches 400+ news syndicated sites and millions of monthly listeners.

✓ A feature interview with YourStory and a database announcement of the winner. yourStory is India's leading entrepreneur site.

✓ $5,000 in services from The Yaffe Group for your blog's logo makeover and matching business cards and stationary.

✓ $5,000+ in an online marketing package from uSocial including targeted traffic of 250,000 YouTube views, 10,000 Facebook followers, 10,000 Twitter followers, 12 months of free press releases.

✓ A feature in Conrad Hall's upcoming book *friends, followers and Customer Evangelists: The 2010 Business Owner's Guide to Social Media.*

✓ Sharing in the prizes for 2nd and 3rd place too.

2nd and 3rd Place - $10,000* Each in Prize Value

✓ A group interview with yourBusinessChanel.com profiling the winners and why you're the best at what you do.

✓ A group interview with Jon Hansen, author and acclaimed online radio host of PI Windows on Business who reaches 1 million monthly syndicated listeners.

✓ A group interview with the new BlogTalkRadio show Game Changers that features professionals who stand above the everyday business crowd.

✓ A group interview on thatchannel.com..

✓ Press releases and notifications announcing the top 3 winners through uSocial, PRInside, Merinews, NewsVine, Twitter, Facebook and LinkedIn giving notice to an audience of over 1.5 million people.

✓ A listing in Conrad Hall's *friends, followers and Customer Evangelists: The 2010 Business Owner's Guide to Social Media.*

✓ The opportunity to join the Community Marketing Blog as an ongoing writer and member of our community.

✓ Announcement of the winners by the judges to their networks and across 1.8 million LinkedIn group members by Andrew Ballenthin.

Why Compete?

1. You want to increase your visibility and leadership position.
2. You want 3rd party verification of your capabilities as a testimonial for your clients or an employer.
3. You want to meet other like minded top professionals and exchange learning.
4. You want to stretch beyond being a solo or corporate blogger and show more people what you can do.
5. You potentially want to join our growing community of writers.

Participants

Names listed in alphabetical order by first name.

Founder

Andrew Ballenthin   President at Sol Solutions
   Blog: http://communitymarketing.typepad.com
   Website: http://www.solsolutions.ca
   LinkedIn: http://ca.linkedin.com/in/andrewballenthin
   Facebook: http://groups.to/socialmediamonetization
   Twitter: http://twitter.com/SolSolutions

Judges

Andrew Jenkins   Principal at Volterra Consulting
   LinkedIn: http://ca.linkedin.com/in/andrewjjenkins
   Twitter: http://twitter.com/ajenkins

Jon Hansen   Host at PI Window on Business Show
 LinkedIn: http://ca.linkedin.com/in/jwhansen
 Twitter: http://twitter.com/piblogger1

Julie Tyios   CEO, Red Juice Marketing
 Website: http://www.julietyios.com
 LinkedIn: http://ca.linkedin.com/in/julietyios
 Twitter: http://twitter.com/julietyios

Mark Sinclair Editor of business tv channel www.ybc.tv
 LinkedIn: http://uk.linkedin.com/in/ybcmark

Mike McClure Exec Creative Director at The Yaffe Group
 LinkedIn: http://www.linkedin.com/in/mikemcclure
 Twitter: http://twitter.com/mikekmcclure

Patrice-Anne Rutledge Author & Communications Consultant
 LinkedIn: http://www.linkedin.com/in/patriceannerutledge
 Twitter: http://twitter.com/patricerutledge

Ted Morris   Managing Director, 4ScreensMedia
 Blog: www.3screenmedia.wordpress.com
 LinkedIn: http://ca.linkedin.com/in/tedmorrissocialmediacrm
 Twitter: http://www.twitter.com/morristed

Sponsors (Prize & Media)
Allan Hoving Social Media Consultant
 LinkedIn: http://www.linkedin.com/in/ahoving

Jim Love   CEO at Chelsea Consulting
 Blog: http://gamechanging.wordpress.com
 Website: http://www.chelseaconsulting.ca
 LinkedIn: http://ca.linkedin.com/in/therealjimlove
 Twitter: http://twitter.com/therealjimlove
 Show: http://BlogTalkRadio.com/GameChanging

Jon Hansen   Host at PI Window on Business Show
 Blog: http://piwindowonbusiness.wordpress.com/
 LinkedIn: http://ca.linkedin.com/in/jwhansen
 Twitter: http://twitter.com/piblogger1

Leon Hill   CEO, uSocial.net
    LinkedIn: http://au.linkedin.com/pub/leon-hill/8/141/68b
    Twitter: http://twitter.com/leonantisocial

Mark Sinclair   Editor of business tv channel www.ybc.tv
    LinkedIn: http://uk.linkedin.com/in/ybcmark

Mike McClure   Exec Creative Director & Social Media Director,
                        The Yaffe Group
    Blog: http://www.yaffetidbitsblog.com
    Website: http://www.yaffe.com
    LinkedIn: http://www.linkedin.com/in/mikemcclure
    Facebook: http://www.facebook.com/#/pages/Southfield-MI/
                The-Yaffe-Group/90846254742
    Twitter: http://twitter.com/mikekmcclure

Shradha Sharma   Founder at Yourstory.in
    LinkedIn: http://in.linkedin.com/pub/shradha-sharma/3/928/807
    Twitter: http://twitter.com/shradhas

Conrad Hall   Chief Copywriter - Conrad Hall
                        Copywriting, LLC
    Blog: http://themarketingspotlight.com
    Website: http://www.theconradhall.com
    LinkedIn: http://www.linkedin.com/in/theconradhall
    Facebook: http://facebook.com/theconradhall
    Twitter: http://twitter.com/TheConradHall

Media Contact

Ginevra Kirkland
    LinkedIn: http://www.linkedin.com/in/ginevra
    Twitter: http://twitter.com/miz_ginevra

Tami Magaro
    Blog: http://www.mindeliverblog.com
    Website: http://www.mindeliver.com
    LinkedIn: http://www.linkedin.com/in/tamimagaro
    Twitter: http://twitter.com/mindeliver

Competitors

Aditya Sinha	http://aditya.sulekha.com/blog/posts.htm
Alison Silbert	http://www.passionateweb.ca/
Catherine Mcquaid	http://www.huntnewbiz.com/
Daina Middleton	http://www.participantmarketing.com
Darlene Sabella	http://darlenesabella.blogspot.com
Elizabeth Thomas	http://msuwordsmith.blogspot.com
Gianluigi Cuccureddu	http://agoramedia.co.uk/blog/social-media/social-media-framework/
Gina Marie Gordon	
Janet Barclay	http://www.janetbarclay.com/
Joanna Wiseberg	http://www.redscarfpromotions.com
Joy Webber	http://balancedworld.com/
Kelly Ann Carpentier	http://www.kellyanncarpentier.com
Laurie Dillon-Schalk	http://socialwisdom.ca/blog/
Lucia Brawley	http://blog.artsusa.org/author/lucia-brawley/
Michael Grosheim	http://blog.harrison-pierce.com
Mike Browne	http://mike-browne.blogspot.com/
Narotam Mangar	http://www.dafilmschool.com
Paritosh Sharma	http://www.proideaz.com
Rick Cordisco	http://activerain.com/blogs/poconorick
Robert Stanke	http://robertstanke.com
Sabrina Gibson	http://www.socialnetworkingrockstar.com
Sam Diener	http://www.samdiener.com/
Sean Nelson	http://www.sonarconnects.com/
Sherry Truhlar	http://www.redappleauctions.com/blog/
Steve Martile	http://www.freedomeducation.ca/
Sue Batton Leonard	http://www.cornerstonefulfillmentservice.com
Therran Oliphant	http://www.fairandbalancedreport.com
Tim Ruffner	http://directmetallasersintering.blogspot.com

YOUR FIRST STEP FOR 2010

Start Your Social Media Marketing
On Autopilot

Have Your:

Blog (Plus Plugins)
Facebook Profile
LinkedIn Profile
Twitter Profile

Set up and connected to each other
Quickly and Easily

Contact Conrad Hall Today
at
conrad@theconradhall.com

You'll have all 4 Ready and Running
In Just Two Business Days

For $199
(That's a 20% discount)

Are you seeking a Workshop Leader for your next Business Event?

Conrad Hall is an author and copywriter working with clients and colleagues in Canada, the U.S., England, France and Australia. He is a vibrant and energetic speaker who combines humor with reliable, useful information.

Workshop Topics

Leadership in Business

Integrating New and Traditional Media for Maximum Effect

As media forms change, business owners are left to wonder where to invest their time, energy and money for advertising. The key to finding the answer isn't with the gurus – it's with your customers. In this workshop, you'll be reminded of the fundamentals because they work. Then you'll see how to apply them to new media so it can be combined with your existing advertising.

Expanding Your Brand with Social Media

You already have a brand – it's based on every interaction a customer has with your business. And people are already talking about you on social media. In this workshop, you'll see how to work with customers, colleagues and even strangers to build and improve your business image (your brand) using social media.

Availability

Workshops can be scaled to fit time slots from one hour to full day. Full day workshops are tailored to suit individual events and cover 2 to 4 topics in addition to those listed.

For multi-day events, more than one presentation can be arranged.

Contact: <u>conrad@theconradhall.com</u>

Ongoing Support for Your Business

Would you like to have a place you can go to find the most up-to-date information about what's working in social media?

How about on-going advice about how to use the Golden Trio sites?

You can have a place where you'll see how to plan and start a group. What it takes to arrange a Tweetup, and which social media sites are growing in market share.

This is the place where I'll be posting monthly updates to this guide, too. After all, it just makes sense to keep track of which sites are growing, which are gone, and when mergers are happening – just like Twitter and LinkedIn joined forces.

That place is www.theconradhall.com.

And what will it cost you to get all this support and information? A whole lot less than you're expecting.

You'll get information submitted from other writers and marketers – people who are getting results from social media every day.

You can also listen to all the recordings from the Voices of Influence program. One hour conversations with business owners and managers who are successfully using social media to grow their businesses.

All for a lot less than you're paying for TV or cell phone every month.

Why is it inexpensive? Two reasons:

1. It has to be accessible to every business owner – even when the budget is tight, and
2. This is the internet age – being able to reach a large audience means we can capitalize on volume marketing. More people involved equals a lower cost for you.

Visit www.theconradhall.com and have a look.

While you're there, be sure to visit www.TheConradHall.com/loyaltycopy for your free digital copy of this book. That way, you can read and highlight the print version while accessing the links and resources in the electronic version (e-book).

More Support for Your Business

SOCIAL MEDIA
VOICES OF INFLUENCE

A Blog Talk Radio Program

http://blogtalkradio.com/theconradhall

**Listen in every Wednesday morning
9:00 am Eastern Time**

✓ Hear business owners, and social media professionals, who are getting real, measurable results with social media.

✓ Listen as they explain what they are doing and how you can put their methods to use for you own business.

Visit:

http://blogtalkradio.com/theconradhall

✓ See the schedule of upcoming shows and access the archive of recorded episodes.

✓ Download any episode and take it with you. You're welcome to play them on your MP3 player, or keep them on CD.

**This content is free.
Please share it with all your friends and colleagues.**

Recommended Reading

Inbound Marketing: Get Found Using Google, Social Media, and Blogs (*Hardcover*)

Brian Halligan, Dharmesh Shah, and David Meerman Scott

To connect with today's buyer, you need to stop pushing your message out and start pulling your customers in. The rules of marketing have changed and the key to winning is to use this change to your advantage.

The New Rules of Marketing and PR (*Paperback*)

David Meerman Scott

Though it may not yet have affected the value of 30 seconds of Super Bowl advertising, PR insider Scott argues that understanding the growing irrelevance of marketing's "old rules" is vital to thriving in the new media jungle.

Naked Conversations (*Hardcover*)

Shel Israel

In this breezy book, Scoble and coauthor Israel argue that every business can benefit from smart "naked" blogging, whether the company's a smalltown plumbing operation or a multinational fashion house. To bolster their argument, Scoble and Israel have assembled an enormous amount of information about blogging: from history and theory to comparisons among countries and industries.

Twitterville *(Hardcover)*

Shel Israel

Social media writer Shel Israel shares revealing stories of Twitterville residents, from CEOs to the student who became the first to report the devastation of the Szechuan earthquake; from visionaries trying to raise money for a cause to citizen journalists who outshine traditional media companies.

Six Pixels of Separation *(Hardcover)*

Mitch Joel

Through the use of timely case studies and fascinating stories, *Six Pixels of Separation* offers a complete set of the latest tactics, insights, and tools that will empower you to reach a global audience and consumer base-and, best yet, you can do this pretty much for free. Digital marketing expert Mitch Joel unravels this fascinating world of new media-but does so with a brand-new perspective that is driven by compelling results.

Trust Agents *(Hardcover)*

Chris Brogan and Julien Smith

Two social media veterans show you how to tap into the power of social networks to build your brand's influence, reputation, and, of course, profits. Today's online influencers are web natives who trade in trust, reputation, and relationships, using social media to accrue the influence that builds up or brings down businesses online.

About the Author

Conrad Hall is an international author, speaker and copywriter. *Friends, followers and Customer Evangelists* is his 5th book.

Conrad's other titles include <u>Starting an Internet Marketing Business after 50</u> (CTC Inc., 2009), <u>The Amazon Instant Bestseller Formula</u> (CTC Inc., 2009), and <u>Writing E-Books for Fun and Profit</u> (CTC Inc., 2008). He is also editor for the AskTaxGuys.com Tax Guide Series.

His copywriting client list includes Accounting and Business Consultants Inc., the Ontario General Contractors Association, March of Dimes Canada, Early To Rise and iRecycle Computers. His focus is working with small and medium size businesses to maximize their return on investment in traditional, online and social media marketing channels.

His current projects include a new book on List Building with Bob Bly, a Blog Talk Radio program titles *Social Media Voices of Influence* (#smvoi), and training his dog Silas to roll-over.

Conrad is available internationally for speaking engagements and via telephone for interviews. His topics include:

- ✓ Leadership in a hyper-connected world
- ✓ Entrepreneurship & Ownership – wedding vision to stamina
- ✓ Career Planning – from carpenter to author and other changes

Please contact Conrad by telephone at 561-623-9441 or e-mail at <u>conrad@theconradhall.com</u>. He has offices in Toronto, ON and Brighton, AL, and currently resides in Illinois.

BUY A SHARE OF THE FUTURE IN YOUR COMMUNITY

These certificates make great holiday, graduation and birthday gifts that can be personalized with the recipient's name. The cost of one S.H.A.R.E. or one square foot is $54.17. The personalized certificate is suitable for framing and will state the number of shares purchased and the amount of each share, as well as the recipient's name. The home that you participate in "building" will last for many years and will continue to grow in value.

Here is a sample SHARE certificate:

YES, I WOULD LIKE TO HELP!

I support the work that Habitat for Humanity does and I want to be part of the excitement! As a donor, I will receive periodic updates on your construction activities but, more importantly, I know my gift will help a family in our community realize the dream of homeownership. **I would like to SHARE in your efforts against substandard housing in my community!** *(Please print below)*

PLEASE SEND ME _____ SHARES at $54.17 EACH = $ $_____

In Honor Of: _____

Occasion: (Circle One)   HOLIDAY   BIRTHDAY   ANNIVERSARY

     OTHER: _____

Address of Recipient: _____

Gift From: _____ *Donor Address:* _____

Donor Email: _____

I AM ENCLOSING A CHECK FOR $ $_____ PAYABLE TO HABITAT FOR HUMANITY <u>OR</u> PLEASE CHARGE MY VISA OR MASTERCARD *(CIRCLE ONE)*

Card Number _____ Expiration Date: _____

Name as it appears on Credit Card _____ Charge Amount $ _____

Signature _____

Billing Address _____

Telephone # Day _____ Eve _____

PLEASE NOTE: Your contribution is tax-deductible to the fullest extent allowed by law.
Habitat for Humanity • P.O. Box 1443 • Newport News, VA 23601 • 757-596-5553
www.HelpHabitatforHumanity.org

LaVergne, TN USA
29 July 2010
191396LV00010B/70/P